John Sarich's
Food & Wine of the
Pacific Northwest

John Sarich

Edited by Robert Spector

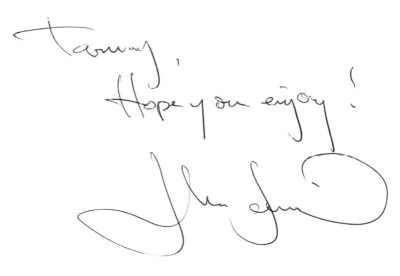

Tammy,
Hope you enjoy!

John Sarich

SASQUATCH BOOKS
SEATTLE

Chateau Ste. Michelle, Woodinville, Washington

For information, write Documentary Book Publishers,
615 Second Avenue, Suite 260, Seattle, WA 98104.

Author: John Sarich
Editor: Robert Spector
Copy Editor: Judy Gouldthorpe
Cover and Book Design: TeamDesign
Illustrator: Karey Manor
Photographer: Darrell Peterson
Project Director: Robin Struyvenberg

Library of Congress Cataloging-in-Publication Data
LC# 93-079327

Sarich, John
John Sarich's Food & Wine of the Pacific Northwest

ISBN 0-935503-11-0

1. Cookbook

2. Recipes—Pacific Northwest

TABLE OF CONTENTS

PACIFIC NORTHWEST CUISINE

Pacific Northwest cuisine is fresh, versatile and highly flavored. It reflects the region's abundance of fresh foods and its multi-ethnic population.

▶ Our geography ranges from the only temperate rain forest in the United States to the high desert plains of the Columbia Valley, which receive less rain than the Mojave Desert. The wheat fields of the Palouse rival any in Kansas, and if you visited the fishing town of Port Townsend you would think you were in New England. ▶ What we cook is dictated by our distinct seasons, which keep our foods interesting and ever-changing. Our cooks look forward to local asparagus, lamb and fresh rosemary in the spring; sweet cherries, strawberries, raspberries, apricots and peaches in the summer; mushrooms, wild game and apples in the fall; and in the winter, the world's best crab, oysters

Native Americans cook salmon with hot green-alder smoke, Swedes bake it, Italians combine it with an assortment of local shellfish to make seafood stew.

and clams. Fresh salmon is available year-round. ▶ Our international cooking style is influenced by those who call this region home, for instance, Native Americans, Mexicans, Scandinavians, French, Chinese, Japanese, Thai, Vietnamese, Italians and, in my case, Croatians. Consequently, every Pacific Northwest chef's approach is different. Native Americans cook salmon with hot green-alder smoke, Swedes bake it, Italians combine it with an assortment of local shellfish to make seafood stew. ▶ The recipes in this cookbook are based on my experience and style, but ultimately, how food is prepared comes down to personal taste and the ingredients and influences in your kitchen. The most important thing to remember is that Pacific Northwest cuisine contains an element of daring, so use your own artistic talents, be bold and have a good time.

ALASKA

BRITISH COLUMBIA

WASHINGTON

OREGON

IDAHO

Chef John Sarich

John Sarich, culinary director of
Chateau Ste. Michelle Winery, is host
of the popular television cooking show
"Taste of the Northwest." ❥ For Sarich,
a native of Seattle, cooking began as a
hobby. "That's why I'm more
comfortable with the term
'cook' than 'chef.'" As well as
being experienced in the ways of
the kitchen, John learned about
the traditions of enology by
helping his father and grandfather make
wine at home. ❥ In 1976, Sarich's life
took a fateful turn when he went on a
picnic at Chateau Ste. Michelle. At the
time, he was proceeding toward a master's
degree in psychology, but he thought it
might be fun to earn a little extra money
during the summer as a winery tour guide.
Sarich stayed, and eventually became
director of winery tours and wine-tasting,

and taught cooking classes that helped promote Chateau Ste. Michelle's wines. He later consulted on behalf of the winery with executive chefs in restaurants all along the Pacific Coast. ❯ In 1980, Sarich fulfilled a lifelong dream when he co-founded the renowned Adriatica Restaurant in Seattle. He was selected by *Esquire* magazine as one of the country's hot new chefs and was named one of the city's top five chefs by *The Seattle Times*. His style, nurtured by his grandparents, who emigrated from the Dalmatian coast of Croatia, is direct, forward and full-flavored. ❯ After establishing a new restaurant, Dalmacija, in Seattle's Pike Place Market, Sarich returned to Chateau Ste. Michelle, where he now creates dishes that are enjoyed by an array of international food and wine personalities who visit the winery in Woodinville.

❯ He is one of the founders of the Center for Northwest Food & Wine Studies, which promotes professional culinary exchanges, chef symposia, seminars and research into the pairing of Pacific Northwest food with the region's wine. He continues to tour the world promoting the virtues of Chateau Ste. Michelle and Pacific Northwest cuisine.

Sarich's style, nurtured by his grandparents, who emigrated from the Dalmatian coast of Croatia, is direct, forward and full-flavored.

CHATEAU STE. MICHELLE

Chateau Ste. Michelle is primarily responsible for establishing the Columbia Valley's reputation as one of the world's great regions for growing vinifera grapes. ❱ Ever since the early 1950s, Chateau Ste. Michelle has been planting classic European grape varieties in its Eastern Washington vineyards, and perfecting growing techniques to take advantage of the Columbia Valley's unique microclimates. Protected from moist Pacific air by the Cascade mountain range, the valley is situated at the same northerly latitude as France's famed vinifera regions of Bordeaux and Burgundy, making it ideally suited for Cabernet Sauvignon, Merlot, Chardonnay and Sauvignon Blanc. ❱ In 1974, Chateau Ste. Michelle earned a spot on the world enological map when its 1972 Johannisberg Riesling was awarded first place in the *Los Angeles Times* Wine Competition against the best Rieslings from Germany and

California. ▶ More recently, wine critic Robert M. Parker, Jr., named Chateau Ste. Michelle to his list of the world's best producers, and he gave the winery's 1983 Cabernet Sauvignon Reserve a 95 rating out of a possible 100. ▶ Mike Januik was named Chateau Ste. Michelle's winemaker in 1990. He was already well known for his 1987 Merlot Reserve and 1987 Cabernet Sauvignon, which made the *Wine Spectator*'s list of the world's 100 best wines. After he joined Chateau Ste. Michelle, his 1990 Sauvignon Blanc was also added to the *Spectator*'s top 100 list. ▶ For Januik, who holds a master's degree in enology from the University of California at Davis, much of winemaking is done by feel or intuition. "As in cooking," he says, "the most important part of winemaking is the ingredients. You need great grapes as well as new French oak barrels for fermentation and aging. . . . The combination of wine and food contains an almost spiritual aspect." ▶ In 1992, Chateau Ste. Michelle announced plans for a new winery, Canoe Ridge Estate, overlooking the Columbia River. Designed for the exclusive production of premium red wine, the winery crushed its first grapes in the fall of 1993.

"As in cooking, the most important part of winemaking is the ingredients."

SPRING

*ON THE PREVIOUS PAGE:
Hood Canal Spot Prawns
with Thai Bean Sauce and
Yakima Valley Asparagus and
Grilled Eggplant with Pesto*

Pacific Northwest seasons have definite character, but where they start and where they end is never precise. April marks the beginning of spring, with warmer days and shorter nights. Signs of freshness and renewal are every-where, as buds burst into flower and herbs come alive. For farmers, it is a time of promise; for cooks, a time of adventure. As we adjust our cooking styles for fresh ingredients, our taste turns to lighter foods with livelier flavors and crisp textures.

As soon as the sun comes out, the tops come down on convertibles and the barbecues emerge in backyards and on balconies. That distinctive grilled flavor changes the character of everything from Copper River salmon to tender, locally raised lamb chops. It is a time for gathering seasonal delicacies such as clams, mussels, deep forest mushrooms and the region's bounty of berries and wild greens. We head over to Fishermen's Terminal, home of Seattle's fishing fleet, for fresh salmon, cold water halibut and a wide selection of white-meat fish. ❱ We start to see Yakima Valley asparagus, which combines wonderfully with grilled eggplant and mayonnaise pesto. Curry asparagus soup with Oregon bay shrimp is an ideal light meal. Near the end of the season, Walla Walla Sweet onions enhance salads and hint at the more bountiful row crops yet to come. ❱ While last year's crush is resting and maturing in the winery, the vine's cycle begins again when daily temperatures rise above 50 degrees Fahrenheit and pollinating bees beget another crop of grapes. The dramatic temperature swings of these dry-land vineyards can range as much as 50 degrees between days and nights, which balances the grapes' sugar and natural acidity.

FRESH IN SPRING

SEAFOOD

Copper River
King Salmon

Prawns

Penn Cove Mussels

Scallops

Shrimp

Clams

Halibut

MEATS

Spring Lamb

Chicken

FRUITS AND VEGETABLES

Spinach

Asparagus

Snap Peas

Lettuce

String Beans

Walla Walla
Sweet Onions

Morels

Herbs

Raspberries

Strawberries

Hood Canal Spot Prawns with Thai Bean Sauce

PRAWNS

1 pack (24) rice flour "tortilla" papers

1 pound prawns (in shells)

½ cup fresh small basil leaves

½ cup fresh mint leaves

½ cup fresh cilantro

3 cups bean sprouts

THAI BEAN SAUCE

2 Tbsp. fermented black beans

½ cup rice wine vinegar

¼ tsp. sesame oil

¼ tsp. hot chili oil

Juice of ½ lemon

3 Tbsp. soy sauce

PRAWNS

Separate and soak rice flour "tortillas" in lukewarm water for ½ hour.

Add prawns to 1 quart boiling water and cook for 3 minutes (until orange).

Drain, cool, then peel, devein and cut in half lengthwise.

In center of each rice paper, place ½ prawn.

Add a few leaves of basil, a sprig of mint and cilantro, and a small amount of bean sprouts.

Fold sides to the center and roll up.

Serve with Thai Bean Sauce for dipping.

THAI BEAN SAUCE

Blend ingredients together.

Let stand at room temperature for 30 minutes.

SERVES: 4
COST: MODERATE
PREPARATION TIME: 30 MINUTES
WINE SUGGESTION: SEMILLON

Yakima Valley Asparagus and Grilled Eggplant with Pesto

Slice eggplants into ½"-thick rounds, drench in olive oil and sauté over medium-high heat until tender.

Blend mayonnaise and pesto and spread on eggplant rounds.

Blanch asparagus in boiling water for 1 minute until bright green, then cool under running water. Drain, then slice in half lengthwise.

On each eggplant round, place one piece of prosciutto and three or four asparagus spear halves.

Roll up and secure with a toothpick.

2 medium eggplants

¼ cup pure olive oil

½ cup mayonnaise

2 Tbsp. Hazelnut Pesto (see recipe, page 48)

½ pound asparagus

½ pound sliced prosciutto

Toothpicks

Serves: 6
Cost: Inexpensive
Preparation time: 30 minutes
Wine suggestion: Sauvignon Blanc

ELLENSBURG LAMB CARPACCIO with HUMMUS

LAMB

2 eight-ounce lamb
loins

4 Tbsp. pure olive oil

1 Tbsp. chopped fresh
rosemary

1 Tbsp. finely chopped
garlic

1 Tbsp. chopped fresh
Italian parsley

½ tsp. coarsely ground
black pepper

2 Tbsp. extra virgin
olive oil

1 package thin-sliced
toasted bread rounds

2 lemons, cut in
wedges

HUMMUS

1 can (8 oz.) garbanzo
beans

Juice of 1 lemon

3 cloves garlic,
chopped

1 tsp. ground cumin

¼ cup sesame paste
(tahini)

Salt

2 Tbsp. chopped fresh
Italian parsley

LAMB

Remove excess fat from lamb loins and
place in large mixing bowl.

Add 2 Tbsp. pure olive oil, rosemary, garlic,
parsley and pepper.

Stir, then cover and let stand for at least
1 hour at room temperature.

In hot heavy skillet, add remaining pure
olive oil, then sear meat 1 minute per side.

Remove loins from pan, cover and let sit in
freezer for 20 minutes, or until firm.

Remove the firm loins from the freezer and
cut across the grain into slices ¼" or thinner.

Drizzle with extra virgin olive oil, then
serve with Hummus, toasted bread rounds
and lemon wedges.

HUMMUS

Drain about ½ of the liquid from can of
garbanzo beans.

Combine garbanzo beans and remaining
liquid, lemon juice, garlic, cumin and
sesame paste in a blender and puree.

Add salt to taste and blend again.

Garnish with chopped parsley.

SERVES: 6
COST: EXPENSIVE
PREPARATION TIME: 45 MINUTES
WINE SUGGESTION: MERLOT

Seafood Caesar Salad with Oregon Blue Cheese

Seafood

Add prawns to 1 quart boiling water and cook until bright orange. Then cool, peel and devein. Add butter and olive oil to a medium-hot sauté pan, then add garlic and sauté until soft.

Add prawns, crab meat and scallops and sauté for 2 minutes.

Sprinkle with pepper flakes, lemon juice and Chardonnay, then simmer for 3 minutes; drain and cool.

Salad and Dressing

Wash, pat dry and tear lettuce into large bite-sized pieces; wrap in cloth towel and store in refrigerator until needed.

Mash garlic in bottom of a bowl; add anchovy paste.

Stir in olive oil, lemon juice, Worcestershire sauce, parsley, dry mustard, sugar and blue cheese and mix until smooth.

Add greens to a large salad bowl, then top with cooled seafood.

Just before serving, add dressing, garlic croutons and tomato wedges; toss, then sprinkle with grated Parmesan cheese.

Serves: 6
Cost: Expensive
Preparation time: 45 minutes
Wine suggestion: Chardonnay

Seafood

½ pound prawns

1 Tbsp. butter

1 Tbsp. pure olive oil

2 cloves garlic, chopped

¼ pound fresh Dungeness crab meat

½ pound scallops

⅛ tsp. red pepper flakes

2 Tbsp. lemon juice

¼ cup Chardonnay

Salad and Dressing

1 head red lettuce

1 head romaine lettuce

2 cloves garlic, chopped

2 anchovy fillets, mashed

⅓ cup extra virgin olive oil

Juice of 1 lemon

Splash of Worcestershire sauce

2 Tbsp. chopped fresh Italian parsley

1 Tbsp. dry mustard

Pinch of sugar

2 Tbsp. Oregon blue cheese, crumbled

1 cup garlic croutons

2 tomatoes, cut in wedges

2 Tbsp. grated Parmesan cheese

Curry Asparagus Soup with Oregon Bay Shrimp

Salt

1 ½ pounds asparagus

2 to 3 cups chicken stock

½ cup sour cream

2 cloves garlic

1 Tbsp. curry powder

1 Tbsp. Semillon

¼ pound small shelled, cooked shrimp

2 red radishes, thinly sliced

Add ½ tsp. salt to 1 quart of boiling water.

Cook asparagus in boiling water until very tender, then cool under cold water.

Combine asparagus, chicken stock, sour cream, garlic, curry powder and Semillon in a blender or food processor.

Puree until very smooth.

Add salt to taste.

Chill and serve, garnished with shrimp and radish slices.

Serves: 4
Cost: Inexpensive
Preparation time: 20 minutes
Wine suggestions: Dry Riesling, Semillon

Penn Cove Mussels and Pasta in Sparkling Wine

Melt butter in a medium-hot high-sided pan (do not brown).

Add onions, shallots and garlic and sauté until very soft and translucent.

Add Sparkling Blanc de Blanc, lemon juice and cream; simmer until reduced by a third.

Stir in lemon zest, tarragon, cayenne pepper and saffron; simmer until thick (about 4 minutes).

While sauce is still bubbling, add mussels; cook until open. (After 3 minutes, discard any unopened mussels.)

Serve over angel hair pasta.

SERVES: 4
COST: INEXPENSIVE
PREPARATION TIME: 30 MINUTES
WINE SUGGESTION: SPARKLING BLANC DE BLANC

4 Tbsp. butter

1 small yellow onion, finely chopped

2 shallots, finely chopped

1 clove garlic, finely chopped

1 cup Sparkling Blanc de Blanc

2 Tbsp. lemon juice

1 pint heavy cream

½ tsp. grated lemon zest

1 Tbsp. chopped fresh tarragon

Pinch of cayenne pepper

Pinch of saffron

2 pounds scrubbed and debearded Penn Cove mussels

1 pound angel hair pasta, cooked and drained

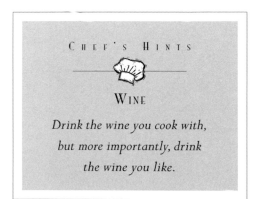

CHEF'S HINTS

WINE

Drink the wine you cook with, but more importantly, drink the wine you like.

WILD MUSHROOM- and THYME-STUFFED RAVIOLI with PARMA CREAM

1 Tbsp. pure olive oil

1 Tbsp. butter

1 cup chopped yellow onion

3 Tbsp. chopped shallots

2 cloves garlic, chopped

1 pound mushrooms, chopped (morel, porcini, Crimini)

1 tsp. dry mustard

½ tsp. lemon juice

¼ cup Sauvignon Blanc

3 – 4 Tbsp. chopped sun-dried tomatoes in oil

2 Tbsp. chopped fresh Italian parsley

1 Tbsp. chopped fresh thyme

½ tsp. coarsely ground black pepper

Salt

PASTA

3 cups flour

1 cup semolina flour

2 extra-large eggs

1 Tbsp. extra virgin olive oil

WILD MUSHROOM FILLING

Add olive oil and butter to a medium-hot frying pan (do not brown).

Sauté onion, shallots and garlic until soft.

Add chopped mushrooms and continue to sauté until soft.

Stir in mustard, lemon juice, Sauvignon Blanc and dried tomatoes.

Simmer until juices evaporate.

Stir in parsley, thyme and pepper.

Salt to taste and cool.

PASTA

Mix flour, semolina, eggs and olive oil and knead until well blended and elastic.

On a lightly floured board, roll out dough to an even thickness of about 1/16".

Cut into 1½" squares.

On half the squares, add mushroom filling, top with remaining squares and press edges together with a fork.

Make 3 filled ravioli for each serving.

Cook ravioli in boiling water for 3 minutes, then drain.

PARMA CREAM

In 2-quart saucepan, bring cream to simmer over medium-low heat (do not boil).

Add butter, Sauvignon Blanc, orange zest, thyme, salt and pepper and reduce until the sauce is very thick.

Stir in prosciutto and serve over ravioli.

Sprinkle with Parmesan cheese.

SERVES: 4
COST: MODERATE, UNLESS YOU KNOW
WHERE TO FIND WILD MUSHROOMS
PREPARATION TIME: 60 MINUTES
WINE SUGGESTIONS: CHARDONNAY,
SAUVIGNON BLANC

PARMA CREAM

4 cups heavy cream

3 Tbsp. butter

1 cup Sauvignon Blanc

¼ tsp. grated
orange zest

1 Tbsp. chopped
fresh thyme

¾ tsp. salt

¼ tsp. white pepper

¼ cup chopped
prosciutto

½ cup grated Parmesan
cheese

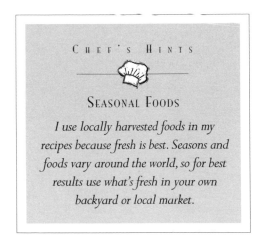

CHEF'S HINTS

SEASONAL FOODS

I use locally harvested foods in my recipes because fresh is best. Seasons and foods vary around the world, so for best results use what's fresh in your own backyard or local market.

Filet Mignon with Cabernet Sauvignon Reduction Sauce

1 Tbsp. pure olive oil

1 Tbsp. butter

4 strips bacon, chopped

3 cups chopped Walla Walla Sweet onions

3 cloves garlic, finely chopped

1 red bell pepper, seeded and coarsely chopped

¼ cup chopped celery tops

½ cup thinly sliced boletus or portobello mushrooms

3 Tbsp. flour

2 Tbsp. tomato paste

2 Tbsp. Worcestershire sauce

2 cups veal stock

2 cups Cabernet Sauvignon

2 Tbsp. chopped fresh rosemary

2 Tbsp. chopped fresh thyme

2 Tbsp. chopped fresh Italian parsley

1 clove

1 bay leaf

¼ tsp. black pepper

Salt

CABERNET SAUVIGNON REDUCTION SAUCE

Add olive oil, butter and bacon to medium-hot sauté pan.

Sauté onions, garlic, bell pepper and celery until very soft.

Cover and simmer over low heat for 15 minutes.

Add mushrooms and sauté until tender.

Sprinkle with flour and stir until absorbed.

Add tomato paste, Worcestershire sauce, veal stock, Cabernet Sauvignon, rosemary, thyme, parsley, clove, bay leaf and pepper.

Stir until well blended, then salt to taste.

Simmer until reduced by a third.

TO BARBECUE — MEDIUM RARE

Pat steaks dry.

Rub in pepper, then salt to taste.

Spread out coals evenly, or set gas-fired grill to medium-high.

Oil grill, then cook steaks for 3 minutes.

Turn and cook 3 more minutes.

Turn the steaks ½ turn to make a cross mark.

Cook 3 minutes.

Turn the steaks over and cross mark on other side for 3 minutes.

Drench with Cabernet Sauvignon Reduction Sauce before serving.

To Saute — Medium Rare

Use a well-seasoned cast iron skillet or nonstick frying pan.

Preheat oven to 325° F.

Pat dry steaks; pepper and salt to taste.

Heat skillet to medium-high, then add olive oil.

Sauté steaks for 2 to 3 minutes on each side.

Then bake in preheated oven for 15 minutes.

Drench with Cabernet Sauvignon Reduction Sauce before serving

SERVES: 4
COST: EXPENSIVE
PREPARATION TIME: 45 MINUTES
WINE SUGGESTION: CABERNET SAUVIGNON

Filet Mignon

4 eight-ounce filet mignon steaks, cut 1½" thick

1 tsp. freshly ground black pepper

Salt

2 Tbsp. pure olive oil

Grilled Ellensburg Lamb Chops with Morel Sauce

2 Tbsp. pure olive oil

¼ pound fresh morels, halved (or substitute Crimini [brown button] mushrooms)

1 large yellow onion, chopped

1 clove garlic, chopped

2 Tbsp. flour

1 cup veal stock

2 Tbsp. Merlot

1 Tbsp. chopped fresh Italian parsley

1 Tbsp. chopped fresh rosemary

1 tsp. dry mustard

½ tsp. grated lemon zest

¼ tsp. freshly ground black pepper

Salt

1 Tbsp. butter

LAMB CHOPS

2 cloves garlic

2 Tbsp. pure olive oil

8 four-ounce lamb chops

¼ tsp. freshly ground black pepper

Salt

MOREL SAUCE

Add olive oil to medium-hot sauté pan and sauté mushrooms, onion and garlic until just soft.

Sprinkle flour over mushroom mixture; continue to sauté for about 2 minutes.

Stir in veal stock, Merlot, parsley, rosemary, mustard, lemon zest and pepper; salt to taste; simmer about 20 minutes.

Just before serving, whisk in butter until completely blended.

LAMB CHOPS

Mash garlic into olive oil.

Rub lamb chops with garlic-olive oil.

Add pepper and salt to taste.

Over medium-hot charcoal or gas fire, grill lamb for about 4 minutes per side.

To serve, spoon about 2 Tbsp. of Morel Sauce over each lamb chop.

SERVES: 4
COST: EXPENSIVE
PREPARATION TIME: 30 MINUTES
WINE SUGGESTION: MERLOT

Grilled Rosemary Garlic Chicken

Combine olive oil, Sauvignon Blanc, lemon juice, rosemary, parsley, garlic, mustard, red pepper flakes and salt to taste.

Add chicken, cover and marinate at room temperature for 1 hour.

Drain excess marinade.

Place chicken, skin side up, over medium-hot charcoal barbecue or gas-fired grill.

Cook at least 15 – 20 minutes.

Turn chicken and cook another 10 – 12 minutes.

Serves: 4
Cost: Moderate
Preparation time: 45 minutes
Wine suggestions: Chardonnay,
Sauvignon Blanc

2 Tbsp. extra virgin olive oil

¼ cup Sauvignon Blanc

Juice of 1 lemon

2 Tbsp. chopped fresh rosemary

2 Tbsp. chopped fresh Italian parsley

3 garlic cloves, chopped

2 tsp. dry mustard

¼ tsp. red pepper flakes, crushed

Salt

1 split broiler chicken

Baked Fresh Halibut with Pesto

4 five-ounce fresh halibut fillets

¼ cup Hazelnut Pesto (see recipe, page 48)

½ cup mayonnaise

1 tsp. lemon juice

2 Tbsp. pure olive oil

Preheat oven to 425° F.

Rinse halibut fillets in fresh water and pat dry.

Mix pesto, mayonnaise and lemon juice; spread over halibut fillets.

Coat a baking dish with olive oil and add the halibut.

Bake for approximately 7 – 10 minutes, or until the fish flakes easily.

SERVES: 4
COST: MODERATE, UNLESS YOU CATCH THE HALIBUT YOURSELF
PREPARATION TIME: 30 MINUTES
WINE SUGGESTIONS: MERLOT, SAUVIGNON BLANC

Grilled Copper River Salmon with Cucumber Dill Sauce

Blend yogurt with lemon juice, dill, garlic, Tabasco, pepper and salt to taste.

Stir yogurt mixture with sliced cucumbers.

Over a medium-hot charcoal or gas fire, grill salmon for approximately 20 minutes, or until fish flakes easily.

Spread yogurt-cucumber mixture over salmon and serve.

Serves: 6
Cost: Moderate
Preparation time: 20 minutes
Wine suggestion: Chardonnay

2 cups plain yogurt

Juice of ½ lemon

1 Tbsp. chopped fresh dill

2 cloves garlic, mashed

Splash of Tabasco

⅛ tsp. white pepper

Salt

½ cucumber, thinly sliced

1 three-pound Copper River salmon fillet

CHINATOWN GINGER BEANS

1 pound fresh snap beans (or green string beans)

1 Tbsp. peanut oil

Splash of sesame oil

Splash of hot chili oil

1 Tbsp. chopped fresh ginger root

2 cloves garlic, chopped

1 Tbsp. seasoned rice wine vinegar

½ tsp. curry powder

1 Tbsp. soy sauce

Blanch beans in boiling water (until bright green).

Drain, then rinse with cold water.

Heat a sauté pan to medium-high, then add peanut, sesame and chili oils.

Add ginger and garlic and sauté until soft.

Add beans and sauté until tender (about 4 minutes).

Sprinkle with rice wine vinegar, curry powder and soy sauce.

Stir and cook for 2 minutes.

SERVES: 4
COST: INEXPENSIVE
PREPARATION TIME: 10 MINUTES

WALLA WALLA SWEET ONIONS and SAUTÉED SPINACH

Add olive oil to medium-hot sauté pan.

Sauté onions and garlic until soft (translucent).

Increase heat to high and add spinach.

Sauté quickly until wilted, then turn off heat.

Add balsamic vinegar and serve hot.

SERVES: 4
COST: INEXPENSIVE
PREPARATION TIME: 10 MINUTES

2 Tbsp. pure olive oil

2 small (green)
Walla Walla Sweet
onions, chopped

1 clove garlic, chopped

2 bunches spinach,
washed, stemmed and
chopped

2 Tbsp. balsamic
vinegar

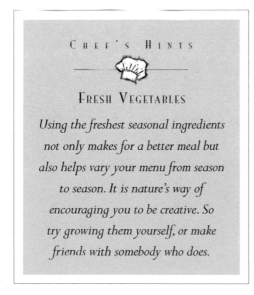

CHEF'S HINTS

FRESH VEGETABLES

Using the freshest seasonal ingredients not only makes for a better meal but also helps vary your menu from season to season. It is nature's way of encouraging you to be creative. So try growing them yourself, or make friends with somebody who does.

PACIFIC NORTHWEST BERRY COMPOTE

1 pint blueberries

1 pint raspberries

1 pint strawberries

1 Tbsp. butter

3 Tbsp. sugar

¼ tsp. grated orange zest

¼ cup Late Harvest White Riesling

1 Tbsp. flour

Clean berries in cold water, then drain.

In a saucepan, melt butter over medium heat, then add sugar, orange zest, Late Harvest White Riesling and flour; whisk until blended.

Add berries and continue to cook until warm throughout.

Serve over rich Vanilla ice cream.

SERVES: 8
COST: INEXPENSIVE
PREPARATION TIME: 10 MINUTES
WINE SUGGESTION: LATE HARVEST WHITE RIESLING

Vashon Island Strawberry Sorbet

Add lemon juice and Late Harvest White Riesling to berries and puree.

Over low heat, melt sugar in water, then let cool.

Mix in berry puree.

Beat egg whites until stiff, then fold into berry puree.

Pour berry mixture into ice cream maker and stir until frozen firm.

2 Tbsp. lemon juice

2 Tbsp. Late Harvest White Riesling

3½ cups fresh strawberries, sliced

½ cup sugar

1 cup water

2 large egg whites

Serves: 4
Cost: Inexpensive
Preparation time: 30 minutes
Wine suggestion: Late Harvest White Riesling

SUMMER

On the Previous Page:
Mixed Grilled Northwest
Vegetable Medley and Hood
River Peach and Nectarine
Ginger Salmon Sauté

Summer never lasts long enough for Pacific Northwest cooks, who spend more time in front of an outdoor barbecue than a kitchen stove. Summer meals—such as bowtie pasta with basil and roasted hazelnuts — are light, but bursting with flavor.

Summer cuisine in the Pacific Northwest is accentuated by such treats as sweet corn still in its husk, Fraser River salmon and razor clams dug out of Pacific Ocean beaches from Alaska to Southern Oregon. If you're like me, you're eating out of your herb garden as much as possible.

For summer salads, few rules apply. We think nothing of combining meats with fruits, or seafood with cheese—blended with backyard-grown tomatoes, fresh herbs, snap peas and marinated green beans. Light dressings are often made with fruit and wine vinegars, honey and olive oil.

While maturing wine grapes in the vineyards are swelled and sweetened by the sun, and colored by night, newly released cold white wines such as Chardonnay, Sauvignon Blanc and Semillon grace outside dining menus. Chilled wines add zest to grilled chicken, salmon or halibut-and-prawn skewers. ❧ The region is best known for its wide variety of fresh short-season fruits. Nothing beats a sun-ripened apricot, unless it's a Pacific Northwest peach or nectarine. For me, summer memories are included in the ingredients of my grandfather's recipe for Yakima River peaches in Cabernet Sauvignon. The sweet, fragrant flavor of the peaches combines with the full flavor of red wine for a lovely finish to a meal. ❧ Fully aware that summer will quickly pass, Pacific Northwest-erners plan ahead. We take out the old family recipes and preserve summer fruits, to be enjoyed in the coming months in the form of stuffings for poultry, toppings for pound cake and fruit jams for Sunday morning toast.

FRESH IN SUMMER

SEAFOOD

Sockeye Salmon

Coho Salmon

Halibut

Razor Clams

Squid

MEATS

Chicken

Lamb

Pork

FRUITS AND VEGETABLES

Cherries

Huckleberries

Apricots

Nectarines

Peaches

Cantaloupe

Grapes

Tomatoes

Leeks

Walla Walla
Sweet Onions

Cucumbers

Bell Peppers

Potatoes

Roasted Sweet Red Pepper Torte

Focaccia Dough

1 package dry yeast

3 cups warm water (95° F)

Pinch of sugar

1 Tbsp. pure olive oil

8 cups bread flour

1 cup semolina flour

1 tsp. salt

Onion Filling

2 Tbsp. pure olive oil

2 large Walla Walla Sweet onions, julienned

2 cloves garlic, chopped

Salt

Sweet Red Pepper

2 red bell peppers

Cheese Topping

8 ounces goat cheese, crumbled

Focaccia Dough (or substitute frozen bread dough)

Mix yeast into water, then add sugar and olive oil and allow to proof 2–3 minutes.

Add flours and salt, then knead until soft, smooth and elastic.

Cover and let rise in a warm, draft-free location until doubled, about 1 hour.

Onion Filling

Heat a heavy skillet to medium-high, then add olive oil and sauté onions and garlic until soft.

Reduce heat to low, cover and continue to cook 25 minutes, stirring occasionally.

Increase heat to medium, remove lid and sauté until lightly browned, then salt to taste.

Sweet Red Pepper

Preheat oven to 350° F.

Quarter and core peppers.

Place each section skin side up on a baking sheet and bake until skin begins to blacken.

Remove from the oven, cool and peel.

Cut into ½"-wide strips.

Preheat oven to 425° F.

Divide focaccia dough into 9 portions, roll into balls and let rise for 20 minutes.

Flatten with rolling pin, place on sheet pans, then make a few deep dents with fingers in the top of each.

Fill with onion mixture, then sprinkle with crumbled goat cheese.

Top with 2 red pepper strips, then bake for 15 minutes, or until browned.

SERVES: 4
COST: INEXPENSIVE
PREPARATION TIME: 75 MINUTES
WINE SUGGESTION: SAUVIGNON BLANC

CHEF'S HINTS

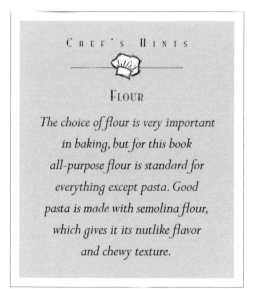

FLOUR

The choice of flour is very important in baking, but for this book all-purpose flour is standard for everything except pasta. Good pasta is made with semolina flour, which gives it its nutlike flavor and chewy texture.

Stone Fruit Salad with Honey Yogurt Dressing

3 peaches

3 nectarines

4 plums

2 Tbsp. lemon juice

1 cup fresh sweet cherries, pitted

1 tsp. grated orange zest

⅛ tsp. nutmeg

½ cup plain yogurt

2 Tbsp. huckleberry honey (or fireweed or wildflower honey)

Fresh mint

Pit, peel and cut peaches, nectarines and plums into wedges.

Place in large salad bowl, sprinkle with lemon juice and mix; add cherries.

Toss with orange zest, then sprinkle with nutmeg.

Blend yogurt with honey, then toss with fruit.

Garnish with fresh mint.

Serves: 4

Cost: Inexpensive

Preparation time: 15 minutes

Wine suggestion: Johannisberg Riesling

Okanogan Goat Cheese Salad with Hazelnuts and Raspberry Vinaigrette

Roasted Hazelnuts

Preheat oven to 350° F.

Place hazelnuts in a pan and bake for 15 minutes; cool slightly.

Vigorously rub the hazelnuts between two dish towels to remove the skins.

Chop coarsely.

Raspberry Vinaigrette

At room temperature, mix together raspberry vinegar, peanut oil, cream, Dijon mustard, lemon zest and sugar.

Salt to taste.

Let stand for 15 minutes before serving.

Salad

Arrange lettuce leaves on a chilled glass plate.

Top with onion rings and tomato wedges.

Sprinkle with crumbled goat cheese and raspberries.

Drizzle the Raspberry Vinaigrette over the salad.

Top with roasted hazelnuts.

Serves: 4
Cost: Inexpensive
Preparation time: 15 minutes
Wine suggestion: Dry Riesling

Roasted Hazelnuts

2 cups hazelnuts

Raspberry Vinaigrette

¼ cup raspberry vinegar

½ cup peanut oil

2 Tbsp. heavy cream

1 Tbsp. Dijon mustard

¼ tsp. grated lemon zest

¼ tsp. sugar

Salt

Salad

2 medium heads Bibb lettuce, washed and dried

1 medium red onion, thinly sliced

2 medium tomatoes, cut in wedges

½ cup crumbled Okanogan goat cheese

¼ pint fresh raspberries

CHILLED PEACH and MELON SOUP

4 peaches

1 large honeydew melon

2 Tbsp. lemon juice

1 tsp. grated orange zest

½ tsp. finely chopped fresh ginger root, plus extra for garnish

1 Tbsp. sugar

½ cup Johannisberg Riesling

Fresh mint leaves

Peel and cube the peaches and melon.

Sprinkle with lemon juice.

Place in blender with orange zest, ginger, sugar and Johannisberg Riesling.

Puree until smooth.

Strain mixture through a medium sieve and refrigerate.

When ready to serve, place in small bowls and garnish with a pinch of fresh ginger and a fresh mint leaf.

SERVES: 4
COST: INEXPENSIVE
PREPARATION TIME: 20 MINUTES
WINE SUGGESTION: JOHANNISBERG RIESLING

Penne with Roma Tomatoes, Fresh Basil and Goat Cheese

Add penne to 1½ quarts boiling salted water, cook for 10 minutes, then drain.

Heat a heavy skillet to medium-high. Add olive oil and sauté onion and garlic until very soft.

Reduce heat to medium, then add tomatoes and cook until soft.

Add Sauvignon Blanc, cover and cook about 5 minutes.

Stir in basil, parsley, anchovies, red pepper flakes, sugar, pepper and salt to taste.

In a large serving dish, toss penne with sauce and top with crumbled goat cheese.

SERVES: 4
COST: INEXPENSIVE
PREPARATION TIME: 30 MINUTES
WINE SUGGESTION: SAUVIGNON BLANC

1 pound penne pasta

2 Tbsp. pure olive oil

1 medium yellow onion, finely chopped

2 cloves garlic, finely chopped

3 cups chopped Roma tomatoes

2 Tbsp. Sauvignon Blanc

¼ cup chopped fresh basil

2 Tbsp. chopped fresh Italian parsley

2 Tbsp. finely chopped anchovies

⅛ tsp. red pepper flakes

⅛ tsp. sugar

½ tsp. finely ground black pepper

Salt

¼ cup crumbled goat cheese

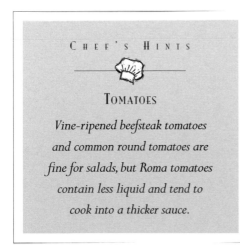

CHEF'S HINTS

TOMATOES

Vine-ripened beefsteak tomatoes and common round tomatoes are fine for salads, but Roma tomatoes contain less liquid and tend to cook into a thicker sauce.

Cold Water Seafood Puttanesca with Sauvignon Blanc

Sauce

½ cup red wine vinegar

3 Tbsp. balsamic vinegar

⅔ cup extra virgin olive oil

4 cups chopped Roma tomatoes

3 cloves garlic, mashed

1 bunch green onions, chopped

1 Tbsp. chopped capers

4 anchovy fillets, chopped

2 Tbsp. sliced green olives

2 Tbsp. chopped celery tops

2 Tbsp. chopped fresh basil

2 Tbsp. chopped fresh Italian parsley

½ tsp. red pepper flakes

1 tsp. dry mustard

1 tsp. coarsely ground black pepper

Salt

Sauce

In a large bowl, mix vinegars, olive oil, tomatoes, garlic, onion, capers, anchovy, olives, celery, basil, parsley, red pepper flakes, mustard, black pepper and salt to taste.

Cover and let stand at room temperature for 1 hour.

Seafood

Heat a large, heavy pot to medium, then add olive oil, lemon juice, Sauvignon Blanc, mussels, clams, scallops and squid.

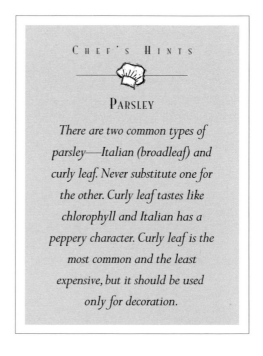

Chef's Hints

Parsley

There are two common types of parsley—Italian (broadleaf) and curly leaf. Never substitute one for the other. Curly leaf tastes like chlorophyll and Italian has a peppery character. Curly leaf is the most common and the least expensive, but it should be used only for decoration.

Reduce heat to low, cover and simmer for 10 minutes, or until mussels and clams open.

Cool slightly, then mix with vegetable sauce.

Linguine

Bring a large pot of lightly salted water and olive oil to a slow boil.

Add linguine and cook for 12 to 15 minutes, then drain and rinse under cold water.

Place linguine over seafood sauce, sprinkle with Parmesan cheese and garnish with sprigs of parsley.

Serves: 4
Cost: Moderate
Preparation Time: 30 minutes
Wine suggestions: Chardonnay, Sauvignon Blanc

Seafood

2 Tbsp. pure olive oil

Juice of ½ lemon

½ cup Sauvignon Blanc

1 pound mussels, cleaned

1 pound clams, cleaned

½ pound scallops

½ pound trimmed squid

Linguine

1 Tbsp. pure olive oil

1 pound dry linguine

¼ cup grated Parmesan cheese

4 sprigs fresh Italian parsley

Roasted Oregon Hazelnut Pesto Pasta

Pasta

1 pound bowtie pasta

Hazelnut Pesto

3 cups tightly packed fresh basil leaves

1 cup tightly packed fresh Italian parsley leaves

4 cloves garlic

1 cup extra virgin olive oil

¼ cup grated Parmesan cheese

2 Tbsp. chopped roasted hazelnuts (see instructions for roasting hazelnuts, page 43)

Salt

Pasta

Boil 1½ quarts salted water in a large pot, then add pasta.

Cook for 10 to 12 minutes, then drain.

Hazelnut Pesto

To a blender or food processor, add basil, parsley, garlic and olive oil a bit at a time and blend until the mixture has a loose paste consistency.

Add cheese and hazelnuts and salt to taste, then blend until smooth.

Mix pesto with pasta and serve warm.

Serves: 4
Cost: Inexpensive
Preparation time: 30 minutes
Wine suggestions: Cabernet Sauvignon, Sauvignon Blanc

Barbecued Lamb Kabobs

At room temperature, combine olive oil, Merlot, garlic, rosemary, parsley, mustard, pepper and salt to taste.

Stir and let stand 15 minutes.

Add lamb cubes to mixture, cover and marinate for 1 hour.

Alternately skewer meat, red pepper and onions.

Over medium-hot coals or gas heat, barbecue the kabobs, turning frequently, for 15 minutes.

Serves: 6
Cost: Moderate
Preparation time: 60 minutes
Wine suggestion: Merlot

¼ cup pure olive oil

½ cup Merlot

4 cloves garlic, mashed

2 Tbsp. chopped fresh rosemary

2 Tbsp. chopped fresh Italian parsley

3 Tbsp. Dijon mustard

½ tsp. medium-grind black pepper

Salt

3 pounds lamb, cut in 1½" cubes

2 red bell peppers, cored and cut into 1" strips

6 small white onions, cut into ¼" slices

CHEF'S HINTS

FRESH HERBS AND GARLIC

With the exception of baking, cooking is not an exact science. Feel free to experiment, using your own taste to adjust the amount of herbs or garlic in any dish.

PICNIC HERBED CHICKEN

½ cup extra virgin
olive oil

2 cloves garlic, smashed

1 frying chicken, cut
into pieces

½ tsp. medium-grind
black pepper

½ tsp. salt

2 cups dry bread
crumbs, crushed fine

2 Tbsp. chopped fresh
rosemary

2 Tbsp. chopped fresh
Italian parsley

2 Tbsp. chopped fresh
oregano

¼ cup grated Parmesan
cheese

Preheat oven to 325° F.

In bowl, mix olive oil and garlic.

Coat chicken with oil, then salt and pepper
to taste.

In a separate bowl, mix bread crumbs,
rosemary, parsley, oregano and Parmesan
cheese.

Dredge oiled chicken in bread crumb mix,
then place in baking dish.

Bake for approximately 20 minutes, then
turn and bake another 20 minutes.

SERVES: 4
COST: MODERATE
PREPARATION TIME: 45 MINUTES
WINE SUGGESTION: CHARDONNAY

Basted Seafood Skewers

Basting Sauce

In a bowl, mix olive oil with Sauvignon Blanc, lemon juice, parsley, tarragon, garlic, mustard, white pepper and salt to taste.

Seafood

Divide halibut, prawns, peppers and onions evenly among skewers.

Place skewers over medium-hot charcoal or gas-fired barbecue, turn and baste frequently with sauce.

Cook 15 minutes, or until halibut and prawns are just done.

Serves: 6
Cost: Moderate to expensive
Preparation time: 45 minutes
Wine suggestion: Sauvignon Blanc

Chef's Hints

Skewers

Soak skewers in cold water 30–60 minutes so they don't burn.

Basting Sauce

¼ cup extra virgin olive oil

½ cup Sauvignon Blanc

Juice of 1 lemon

¼ cup chopped fresh Italian parsley

2 Tbsp. chopped fresh tarragon

4 cloves garlic, mashed

½ tsp. dry mustard

½ tsp. finely ground white pepper

Salt

Seafood

1½ pounds halibut fillet, cut into 1" cubes

12 prawns, shelled and deveined

3 red bell peppers, cored and cut into 1" squares

3 yellow or green bell peppers, cored and cut into 1" squares

2 medium yellow onions, cut into 1" squares

6 long bamboo skewers

Hood River Peach and Nectarine Ginger Salmon Sauté

PEACH/NECTARINE SAUCE

2 Tbsp. peanut oil

1 red onion, chopped

2 shallots, chopped

4 peaches, peeled, pitted and coarsely chopped

2 nectarines, peeled, pitted and coarsely chopped

2 Tbsp. chopped fresh cilantro

1 tsp. finely chopped fresh ginger root

2 cloves

Juice of 1 lime

¼ cup Chardonnay

2 Tbsp. apple juice

Pinch of red pepper flakes

½ tsp. medium-grind black pepper

Salt

SALMON

2 pounds salmon fillet or 4 eight-ounce salmon steaks

2 Tbsp. pure olive oil

½ tsp. medium-grind black pepper

Salt

1 small green alder branch, cut up with leaves on

PEACH/NECTARINE SAUCE

Heat a heavy skillet to medium-high, add peanut oil, then quickly sauté onion and shallots until hot (not soft).

Reduce heat to medium, then stir in peaches, nectarines, cilantro, ginger, cloves, lime juice, Chardonnay, apple juice, red pepper flakes and black pepper; salt to taste.

Bring sauce to a boil, then remove and cool.

Sauce can also be used with chicken.

SALMON

Rinse and pat salmon dry; oil, pepper and salt to taste.

Heat charcoal or gas-fired grill to medium-high, then quickly add alder directly on top of coals or into smoke box of gas-fired grill.

Place the salmon, skin side down, on grill and cover.

Cook for 12 to 15 minutes, or until salmon just flakes.

Serve with Peach/Nectarine Sauce.

SERVES: 4
COST: MODERATE, UNLESS YOU CATCH YOUR OWN SALMON
PREPARATION TIME: 20 MINUTES
WINE SUGGESTION: CHARDONNAY

Grilled Pacific Ocean Ahi Tuna with Cilantro Pesto

Cilantro Pesto

In a blender or food processor, combine cilantro leaves, green onions, garlic, chili powder, cayenne pepper, lime juice, olive oil and green chilies, then blend until smooth.

Add salt to taste and blend again.

Tuna

Rinse and dry tuna, then rub with oil.

Sprinkle with white pepper and salt to taste.

Over charcoal or gas barbecue heated to medium-high, cook tuna for no more than 4 minutes per side.

Garnish with Cilantro Pesto.

Serves: 4
Cost: Moderate
Preparation time: 20 minutes
Wine suggestion: Chardonnay

Cilantro Pesto

1 large bunch cilantro

2 bunches green onions, chopped

3 cloves garlic

1 tsp. chili powder

Pinch of cayenne pepper

Juice of 2 limes

½ cup extra virgin olive oil

1 small can chopped green chilies

Salt

Tuna

4 six-ounce tuna steaks or fillets

2 Tbsp. pure olive oil

½ tsp. finely ground white pepper

Salt

BEANS and QUINCY RED POTATOES

6 medium red potatoes

1 quart chicken stock or water

3 fresh sage leaves

1 clove garlic, mashed

½ tsp. salt

1 pound fresh green beans, cleaned and broken in half

2 Tbsp. extra virgin olive oil

½ tsp. freshly ground black pepper

Boil potatoes in stock (or water) with sage, garlic and salt until soft.

Add beans, cover and cook until beans are bright green and tender (not crunchy).

Drain liquid, then thoroughly mix in olive oil and pepper (potatoes should break apart a little).

SERVES: 4
COST: INEXPENSIVE
PREPARATION TIME: 30 MINUTES

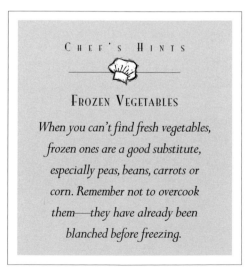

CHEF'S HINTS

FROZEN VEGETABLES

When you can't find fresh vegetables, frozen ones are a good substitute, especially peas, beans, carrots or corn. Remember not to overcook them—they have already been blanched before freezing.

Mixed Grilled Northwest Vegetable Medley

In a large bowl, mix olive oil with lemon juice, parsley, garlic, Sauvignon Blanc and pepper, then salt to taste.

Dip vegetables in olive oil mixture, then cook over medium-high charcoal or gas barbecue, basting frequently, until just tender.

Serves: 4
Cost: Inexpensive
Preparation time: 15 minutes

½ cup pure olive oil

Juice of 1 lemon

¼ cup chopped fresh Italian parsley

4 cloves garlic, mashed

2 Tbsp. Sauvignon Blanc

½ tsp. finely ground black pepper

Salt

4 medium zucchini, cut lengthwise ½" thick

2 Walla Walla Sweet onions, sliced ½" thick

2 red bell peppers, cored and halved

1 yellow bell pepper, cored and halved

1 pound large mushrooms

1 eggplant, sliced ½" thick

Whidbey Island Loganberry Pie

4 cups Whidbey Island loganberries, rinsed and drained

1 cup sugar

¼ cup packed brown sugar

¼ tsp. grated orange zest

⅓ cup flour

2 Tbsp. Whidbeys Loganberry Liqueur

Crust for a 9-inch pie, or puff pastry dough for turnovers

1 Tbsp. sugar

Egg Wash

1 egg whipped with ¼ cup water

Preheat oven to 425° F.

Put berries in a bowl, then gently stir in white and brown sugars, orange zest, flour and liqueur, mixing thoroughly.

For Pie

Fill bottom crust, egg-wash the edges, then add top crust and press down edges with fork.

Slit or perforate top crust, then egg-wash and lightly sugar.

Bake for 10 minutes, then reduce heat to 350° F.

Bake another 20 minutes, or until the crust is golden brown.

For Turnovers

Cut pastry dough into 3" squares.

Place 2 or 3 Tbsp. of berries in center of each square, then fold and press the edges together.

Perforate with a fork.

Bake for 10 minutes, then reduce heat to 350° F.

Continue baking for another 20 minutes, or until the pastry is lightly browned.

Serves: 6
Cost: Inexpensive
Preparation time: 50 minutes
Wine suggestion: Late Harvest White Riesling

Yakima River Peaches in Cabernet Sauvignon

This is the way my grandfather would lovingly treat peaches.

Place the peach slices in the wine glasses and fill with Cabernet Sauvignon.

Let stand at room temperature for 20 to 30 minutes, then garnish with a sprig of fresh mint and serve with biscotti.

4 peaches, peeled, pitted and sliced

4 wine glasses

1 bottle Cabernet Sauvignon

Fresh mint sprigs

1 dozen biscotti

SERVES: 4
COST: INEXPENSIVE
PREPARATION TIME: 15 MINUTES
WINE SUGGESTION: CABERNET SAUVIGNON

FALL

On the Previous Page:
Wild Duck with
Cabernet Sauvignon
Chukar Cherry Sauce

When the days grow short and the nights turn cool in the Pacific Northwest, menus become more complex, and red wines such as Cabernet Sauvignon or Merlot are popular. In fall, the variety of local food is no less abundant than in spring and summer, just different.

The reproductive cycles of local shellfish influence their flavor and texture. In the fall, Hood Canal spot prawns and oysters become tighter and firmer, as do saltwater fish such as rockfish, salmon and lingcod. Wild bounty—from deer, duck and pheasant to chanterelle mushrooms—is a unique part of the Pacific Northwest cuisine in the traditional fall hunting season. Two of my favorite wild poultry dishes are duck breast with Cabernet Sauvignon and Chukar cherries, and Canoe Ridge pheasant breast stuffed with sage and chanterelle sauce. Seasonal abundance is apparent. Dinner tables are vibrant with Yakima Valley lentil soup; hot seafood gazpacho;

Cascade Mountain wild mushroom salad; Idaho and Washington potatoes; and a variety of rich desserts that we only fantasized about during bathing suit season. A Merlot that complements a fall dinner, and a rich port for dessert, are ample compensation for the shorter days and cooler nights.

In the vineyard, by late September or early October, about 100 days after the flowering, it is time to pick the mature, sweetened grape clusters. The harvest begins in the coldness of night in order to preserve the grapes' freshness on their journey to the winery, where they are immediately crushed. Then the juice is fermented, aged, blended and cellared until the wine's release.

FRESH IN FALL

SEAFOOD

Salmon

Ling Cod

Rockfish

Scallops

Alaskan Spot
Prawns

Dungeness Crab

MEATS

Pheasant

Duck

Goose

Venison

FRUITS AND VEGETABLES

Yellow Onions

Peppers of all kinds

Chanterelles

Lentils

Squash

Grapes

Apples

Pears

Stuffed Pacific Squid

1 pound squid, cleaned (save the tentacles)

1 cup chopped fresh spinach, cooked and squeezed dry

½ cup grated Parmesan cheese

2 Tbsp. extra virgin olive oil

¼ cup fine dry bread crumbs

2 Tbsp. chopped shallots

2 cloves garlic, mashed

8 slices of prosciutto, finely chopped

Juice of ½ lemon

¼ cup Sauvignon Blanc

Pinch of cayenne pepper

½ tsp. ground white pepper

Salt

2 Tbsp. pure olive oil

Sweet Red Pepper Puree

2 Tbsp. pure olive oil

2 red bell peppers, cored and thinly sliced

2 large yellow onions, thinly sliced

3 cloves garlic, chopped

½ tsp. red pepper flakes

Salt

Stuffed Squid

Chop squid tentacles, then combine with spinach, Parmesan cheese, olive oil, bread crumbs, shallots, garlic, prosciutto, lemon juice, Sauvignon Blanc, cayenne pepper, white pepper and salt to taste. Mix thoroughly.

Stuff the squid bodies and secure with a toothpick.

Add olive oil to a medium-hot frying pan and sauté the stuffed squid about 1½ minutes per side.

Serve with Sweet Red Pepper Puree for dipping.

Sweet Red Pepper Puree

Add olive oil to a frying pan heated to medium, then sauté peppers, onion and garlic, seasoning with pepper flakes and salt to taste.

Reduce heat to low and cook, stirring occasionally, until very soft, about 30 minutes.

Puree in blender.

Serves: 6
Cost: Inexpensive to moderate
Preparation time: 60 minutes
Wine suggestion: Sauvignon Blanc

STEAMED SAN JUAN BUTTER CLAMS in HERBED OLIVE OIL WINE SAUCE

Soak clams in cold salted water for 1 hour, then drain.

Heat large pot to medium; add olive oil, garlic, parsley, rosemary, pepper flakes, lemon juice and Sauvignon Blanc.

When the mixture begins to boil, add clams.

Cover and cook over high heat for 7 minutes, or until clams open.

Shake pot occasionally, as you would popcorn.

Discard any shellfish that remains unopened after cooking.

4 pounds small butter clams

2 Tbsp. extra virgin olive oil

4 cloves garlic, chopped

2 Tbsp. chopped fresh Italian parsley

1 Tbsp. chopped fresh rosemary

Pinch of red pepper flakes

Juice of 1 lemon

¼ to ½ cup Sauvignon Blanc

SERVES: 4
COST: INEXPENSIVE
PREPARATION TIME: 15 MINUTES
WINE SUGGESTION: SAUVIGNON BLANC

CHEF'S HINTS

OLIVE OIL

Use extra virgin in salads, marinades and pasta or as a topping for bread. Use pure olive for hot frying or sautés, and always bring your sauté pan or skillet up to temperature before adding oil or butter.

Warm Cascade Mountain Wild Mushroom Salad

1 pound chanterelles

½ pound oyster mushrooms

½ pound black trumpet mushrooms (if available)

½ pound morel mushrooms

2 Tbsp. pure olive oil

1 medium yellow onion, chopped

1 red bell pepper, cored and diced

2 cloves garlic, finely chopped

1 Tbsp. chopped fresh thyme

2 Tbsp. chopped fresh Italian parsley

2 Tbsp. sherry vinegar

Pinch of red pepper flakes

1 tsp. dry mustard

Freshly ground black pepper

Salt

Coarsely chop the mushrooms.

In a medium-hot sauté pan, heat olive oil and sauté onion and red pepper until tender.

Increase heat to high, then add garlic and mushrooms.

Sauté quickly until just tender, then remove from heat.

Stir in thyme, parsley, vinegar, red pepper flakes, mustard, and pepper and salt to taste.

Serve on toasted slices of french bread or focaccia (see recipe, page 40).

Serves: 4 to 6
Cost: Expensive
Preparation time: 60 minutes
Wine suggestion: Chardonnay

"Hot" Northwest Seafood Gazpacho

Add olive oil to a medium-hot pan (a high-side sauté pan or heavy 6-quart pot), then sauté onion and garlic for 5 minutes; add tomatoes, cilantro and basil, and season with chili powder, pepper flakes and salt to taste.

Add lemon juice, Chardonnay, tomato sauce and chicken stock, then simmer (uncovered) for 10 minutes.

Add scallops, salmon and prawns and cook until prawns turn color, about 4 minutes. Do not overcook.

SERVES: 4
COST: MODERATE
PREPARATION TIME: 60 MINUTES
WINE SUGGESTION: CHARDONNAY

2 Tbsp. pure olive oil

½ cup chopped onion

2 cloves garlic, finely chopped

3 cups chopped tomatoes

2 Tbsp. chopped fresh cilantro

2 Tbsp. chopped fresh basil

2 Tbsp. chili powder

Pinch of red pepper flakes

Salt

Juice of ½ lemon

¼ cup Chardonnay

1 can (16-oz.) tomato sauce

2 cups chicken stock

¼ pound scallops

¼ pound salmon chunks

½ pound prawns, shelled and deveined

Yakima Valley Lentil Soup

2 Tbsp. pure olive oil

1 cup chopped red bell pepper

1 cup chopped yellow bell pepper

2 cups chopped yellow onion

4 cloves garlic, chopped

1 fennel bulb, chopped

6 cups chicken stock

1 cup Cabernet Sauvignon

1 ham hock

2 Tbsp. chopped fresh oregano

1 Tbsp. chopped fresh Italian parsley

2 bunches Swiss chard, chopped

2 cups lentils

1 tsp. ground cumin

Pinch of red pepper flakes

½ tsp. freshly ground black pepper

Salt

Heat a large pot over medium heat, add olive oil and sauté red and yellow peppers, onion, garlic and fennel until soft.

Pour in stock and Cabernet Sauvignon, then add ham hock, oregano, parsley, Swiss chard and lentils.

Season with cumin, red pepper flakes, black pepper and salt to taste, then reduce heat to low.

Cover and simmer for 1 hour, stirring occasionally.

SERVES: 6
COST: INEXPENSIVE
PREPARATION TIME: 30 MINUTES
WINE SUGGESTION: CABERNET SAUVIGNON

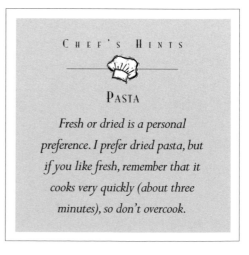

CHEF'S HINTS

PASTA

Fresh or dried is a personal preference. I prefer dried pasta, but if you like fresh, remember that it cooks very quickly (about three minutes), so don't overcook.

HOOD CANAL CLAM PASTA

Heat a large sauté pan to medium–high, then add pure olive oil.

Sauté red pepper, onions and garlic until soft.

Add tomatoes and simmer until soft, then add celery leaves, 2 Tbsp. parsley and basil. Stir in ½ cup Sauvignon Blanc, reduce heat to low and cook for 30 minutes, stirring occasionally, until thick.

Pour remaining Sauvignon Blanc and extra virgin olive oil into a separate large pot over medium heat and bring to a simmer.

Add clams, lemon juice, rosemary and red pepper flakes.

Steam until clams open, then cool. Reserve 1 cup of clam broth.

Remove clams from shells, then chop clam meat.

Add chopped clams and 1 cup of the clam broth to the tomato sauce; simmer for 10 minutes.

Spoon clam sauce over linguine and garnish with Parmesan and the remaining parsley.

Serves: 6
Cost: Moderate
Preparation time: 60 minutes
Wine suggestion: Sauvignon Blanc

2 Tbsp. pure olive oil

1 red bell pepper, cored and thinly sliced

3 cups onions, thinly sliced

4 large cloves garlic, chopped

3 cups seeded, peeled and chopped plum tomatoes

¼ cup chopped celery leaves

¼ cup chopped fresh Italian parsley

2 Tbsp. chopped fresh basil

¾ cup Sauvignon Blanc

3 Tbsp. extra virgin olive oil

5 pounds steamer clams, cleaned

Juice of 1 lemon

2 Tbsp. chopped fresh rosemary

½ tsp. crushed red pepper flakes

1 pound linguine, cooked and drained

¼ cup grated Parmesan cheese

Autumn Mushroom Pasta Pappardelle

4 Tbsp. pure olive oil

1 large yellow onion, coarsely chopped

2 cloves garlic, chopped

2 Tbsp. chopped celery leaves

1 Tbsp. tomato paste

2 cups veal stock

2 Tbsp. Sauvignon Blanc

¾ pound portobello, chanterelle or morel mushrooms, sliced

2 Tbsp. chopped fresh Italian parsley

½ tsp. medium-grind black pepper

4 large fresh sage leaves

1 Tbsp. butter

Salt

½ pound pappardelle noodles, cooked and drained

¼ cup Parmesan cheese

Add 2 Tbsp. olive oil to a medium-hot sauté pan and sauté onion until soft.

Cover, turn heat to low and simmer for at least 20 minutes, stirring occasionally.

Stir in garlic and simmer 5 minutes.

Add celery leaves and tomato paste and mix well, then add veal stock and Sauvignon Blanc and simmer until sauce is reduced by a third.

To a separate sauté pan heated to high, add 2 Tbsp. olive oil; sauté sliced mushrooms until soft (if they brown a bit, all the better).

Add the onion sauce, parsley, pepper and sage.

Simmer over medium-low heat for 5 minutes.

Finish the sauce by stirring in butter, then salt to taste.

Toss pappardelle with sauce, then sprinkle with Parmesan cheese.

SERVES: 4
COST: MODERATE
PREPARATION TIME: 45 MINUTES
WINE SUGGESTIONS: MERLOT, SAUVIGNON BLANC

Ossobucco

Lightly dredge veal shanks in flour.

Add olive oil to a medium-hot heavy pot.

Brown the bacon, then add the veal shanks.

Brown on both sides and remove the shanks.

In the same pan, sauté onion, fennel, bell pepper, garlic and celery until very tender.

Add tomatoes, cover and simmer 10 minutes.

Then add parsley, rosemary, thyme, bay leaves, orange zest, clove and nutmeg. Mix thoroughly.

Add tomato paste, veal stock, Cabernet Sauvignon and sugar.

Simmer 5 minutes, then add veal shanks and cover.

Cook over low heat for 1 hour, or in a 350° F oven for 90 minutes, or until meat is very tender. Stir occasionally.

Serves: 4
Cost: Moderate
Preparation time: 1½ hours
Wine suggestion: Cabernet Sauvignon

2 veal shanks (1½ pounds each), cut in 1½" slices

½ cup flour

2 Tbsp. pure olive oil

¼ cup chopped bacon or pancetta

2 onions, julienned

1 fennel bulb, finely chopped

1 red bell pepper, cored and chopped

4 cloves garlic, finely chopped

½ cup chopped celery tops

4 cups chopped Roma tomatoes

2 Tbsp. chopped fresh Italian parsley

3 Tbsp. chopped fresh rosemary

3 Tbsp. chopped fresh thyme

2 bay leaves

1 tsp. grated orange zest

1 clove

¼ tsp. grated nutmeg

1 Tbsp. tomato paste

1 cup veal stock

½ cup Cabernet Sauvignon

Pinch of sugar

Pork Tenderloin with Raisins and Oregon Hazelnuts

2 large pork tenderloins (about 1½ pounds total)

½ cup flour

½ tsp. salt

½ tsp. finely ground black pepper

2 Tbsp. pure olive oil

1 yellow onion, cut very thin

2 shallots, finely chopped

1 clove garlic, mashed and chopped

¼ cup Dry Riesling

2 Tbsp. chopped roasted hazelnuts (see instructions for roasting hazelnuts, page 43)

¼ cup Sultana (golden) raisins, soaked in red wine vinegar for 20 minutes

⅛ tsp. dry mustard

1 tsp. chopped fresh Italian parsley

1 tsp. chopped fresh thyme

Pinch of cayenne pepper

Pinch of grated lemon zest

1 Tbsp. balsamic vinegar

Parsley sprigs

Cut pork tenderloins into ¾" slices and gently pound to about ½" thickness.

Dredge in a mixture of flour, salt and pepper.

Add olive oil to a hot heavy skillet.

Quickly brown pork on both sides, then remove to warm platter.

In the same pan sauté onion, shallots and garlic until just soft (do not brown).

Add Dry Riesling, then hazelnuts, drained raisins, mustard, parsley, thyme, cayenne pepper, lemon zest and vinegar and simmer for 2 to 3 minutes (until sauce thickens).

Spoon sauce over pork and garnish with sprigs of parsley.

Serves: 4 to 6
Cost: Moderate
Preparation time: 60 minutes
Wine suggestion: Dry Riesling

Wild Duck with Cabernet Sauvignon Chukar Cherry Sauce

Pierce the skin side of each breast with a fork (all over the breast), then season with salt and pepper.

Add olive oil to a hot heavy skillet, then brown the breasts skin side down (to render excess fat) for 3 minutes.

Turn, brown the other sides for 1 minute, then remove breasts to drain.

Reduce heat to medium-high, drain off all but 1 Tbsp. of duck fat, then sauté onion and garlic until soft.

Add veal stock, Cabernet Sauvignon, celery, rosemary, parsley, nutmeg, Chukar cherries, sugar and tomato paste.

Bring to a boil, add pepper and salt to taste, and simmer until sauce is reduced by a third.

Add duck breasts to sauce and simmer, covered, for 20 minutes.

Remove breasts and slice ⅜" thick.

Pour sauce over angel hair pasta, top with sliced duck and garnish with chopped radicchio.

SERVES: 4
COST: EXPENSIVE, UNLESS YOU SHOOT IT YOURSELF
PREPARATION TIME: 60 MINUTES
WINE SUGGESTIONS: CABERNET SAUVIGNON, MERLOT

4 duck breasts, boned, with skin on

Salt

Freshly ground black pepper

2 Tbsp. pure olive oil

1 large onion, thinly sliced

2 cloves garlic, chopped

1 cup veal stock

1 cup Cabernet Sauvignon

1 Tbsp. chopped celery leaves

1 tsp. chopped fresh rosemary

1 Tbsp. chopped fresh Italian parsley

⅛ tsp. grated nutmeg

½ cup Chukar cherries (dried and pitted)

Pinch sugar

1½ Tbsp. tomato paste

½ tsp. freshly ground black pepper

Salt

½ pound angel hair pasta, cooked and drained

Finely chopped radicchio

CANOE RIDGE
PHEASANT BREAST with
CHANTERELLE SAUCE

3 Tbsp. butter

2 Tbsp. fine dry bread crumbs

2 tsp. chopped fresh sage

½ tsp. dry mustard

½ tsp. white pepper

Salt

4 pheasant breasts with wings and skin on

2 Tbsp. flour

3 Tbsp. pure olive oil

2 Tbsp. chopped shallots

½ pound sliced chanterelle mushrooms

¼ cup Chardonnay

¼ cup chicken stock

Juice of ½ lemon

¼ tsp. paprika

¼ tsp. cayenne pepper

¼ tsp. finely ground black pepper

Salt

1 Tbsp. cognac

Mix 2 Tbsp. butter with bread crumbs, 1 tsp. sage, mustard, pepper and salt to taste.

Make a small incision on the side of each breast and place about 1 Tbsp. of the herbed bread crumbs into the opening; pat closed.

Dust the breasts with 1 Tbsp. flour.

In a heavy skillet heated to medium, add 1 Tbsp. butter and 1 Tbsp. olive oil, then lightly brown pheasant breasts on both sides.

Remove breasts from skillet and keep warm.

Increase skillet heat to medium-high, add the remaining olive oil, and sauté shallots and mushrooms until wilted.

Sprinkle remaining flour over mushrooms and continue to sauté until slightly browned around the edges.

Reduce heat to medium, then add Chardonnay, chicken stock, lemon juice, paprika, 1 tsp. sage, cayenne pepper, black pepper and salt to taste.

Simmer until sauce thickens, then finish with cognac.

Spoon over pheasant breasts just before serving.

SERVES: 4
COST: EXPENSIVE WITH PHEASANT, INEXPENSIVE WITH CHICKEN
PREPARATION TIME: 60 MINUTES
WINE SUGGESTIONS: CHARDONNAY, MERLOT

Chicken Breasts in Washington State Apple Cream Sauce

Wash chicken, pat dry and dredge in flour.

Heat a heavy skillet to medium–high and add butter.

Place chicken in melted butter skin side down and gently brown, about 8 minutes on each side, then remove.

In the same pan, sauté onion, apple and garlic until quite soft.

Reduce heat to medium, then add Chardonnay, lemon juice, raisins, pepper and salt to taste. Simmer for 5 minutes.

Add rosemary and cream, stirring until well blended.

Return chicken to pan, cover and cook over low heat, turning occasionally, for 25 minutes.

Remove chicken to serving plate and reduce sauce slightly.

Pour sauce over chicken and garnish with chopped roasted hazelnuts.

4 chicken breast halves

½ cup flour

3 Tbsp. butter

¼ cup thinly sliced onion

¼ cup peeled, julienne-sliced Granny Smith apple

1 clove garlic, mashed

¼ cup Chardonnay

Squeeze of lemon

2 Tbsp. golden raisins

¼ tsp. finely ground white pepper

Salt

1 Tbsp. chopped fresh rosemary

¼ cup heavy cream

¼ cup chopped roasted hazelnuts (see instructions for roasting hazelnuts, page 43)

SERVES: 4
COST: MODERATE
PREPARATION TIME: 60 MINUTES
WINE SUGGESTION: CHARDONNAY

Herb–Marinated Chinook Salmon

1 Tbsp. extra virgin olive oil

2 Tbsp. Chardonnay

Juice of ½ lemon

2 Tbsp. chopped fresh Italian parsley

2 Tbsp. chopped fresh basil

2 cloves garlic, finely chopped

2 Tbsp. chopped shallots

½ tsp. paprika

2 Tbsp. capers

1 Tbsp. dry mustard

½ tsp. finely ground white pepper

Salt

4 six-ounce salmon fillets

½ cup fine dry bread crumbs

2 Tbsp. butter

2 Tbsp. pure olive oil

4 sprigs Italian parsley

In large baking dish, mix together extra virgin olive oil, Chardonnay, lemon juice, parsley, basil, garlic, shallots, paprika, capers, dry mustard, pepper and salt to taste.

Place salmon in marinade for no more than 20 minutes.

Remove salmon and dredge in bread crumbs (reserve marinade).

To a medium-hot skillet, add butter and pure olive oil, then quickly sauté fillets until browned on both sides (about 3 minutes per side) and remove to a warm serving platter.

To the same pan add the remaining marinade and bring to a boil. Pour over salmon fillets.

Garnish with parsley.

SERVES: *4*
COST: *MODERATE*
PREPARATION TIME: *30 MINUTES*
WINE SUGGESTION: *CHARDONNAY*

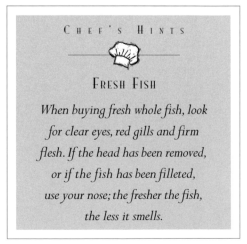

CHEF'S HINTS

FRESH FISH

When buying fresh whole fish, look for clear eyes, red gills and firm flesh. If the head has been removed, or if the fish has been filleted, use your nose; the fresher the fish, the less it smells.

Westport Crab and Shrimp Cannelloni with Hazelnut Pesto

Stuffing

In a blender or food processor, puree olive oil with roasted red peppers.

Add crab, shrimp, garlic, Romano cheese, parsley, Chardonnay, pepper and salt to taste and blend gently.

Cannelloni

Preheat oven to 325° F.

In 2 quarts boiling water, cook four 2½"- to 3"-wide sheets of pasta very al dente, then rinse under cold running water and lay flat.

Thinly spread seafood mixture over pasta and roll up.

Place in buttered baking dish.

Add a small amount of your favorite tomato sauce or marinara sauce around pasta, then bake for 10–12 minutes, or until heated through.

Cut cannelloni into 1½" widths.

Spread Hazelnut Pesto on plates and top with sliced cannelloni.

Serves: 4
Cost: Expensive, unless you know a crabber
Preparation time: 1½ hours
Wine suggestion: Chardonnay

Stuffing

2 Tbsp. extra virgin olive oil

1 cup roasted red pepper strips (see instructions for roasting peppers, page 40)

1 pound Dungeness crab meat

1 pound cooked shrimp, chopped

1 clove garlic, finely chopped

¼ cup grated Romano cheese

1 Tbsp. chopped fresh Italian parsley

Splash of Chardonnay

¼ tsp. freshly ground black pepper

Salt

Cannelloni

For pasta recipe, see page 22.

Tomato or Marinara Sauce

Use your favorite.

Hazelnut Pesto

See recipe, page 48.

Russet Potatoes
with Roasted Garlic
and Basil

1 whole garlic bulb

2 Tbsp. extra virgin olive oil

½ tsp. freshly ground black pepper

½ tsp. salt

4 medium russet potatoes, peeled and boiled soft

3 Tbsp. chopped fresh basil

2 Tbsp. heavy cream

2 Tbsp. butter

2 Tbsp. grated Parmesan cheese

Salt and pepper

Preheat oven to 325° F.

Clean loose skin from outer garlic cloves—but leave bulb whole—then cut off the top ⅛" of the garlic bulb.

Rub bulb with 1 Tbsp. olive oil, then season with pepper and salt.

Place in small ovenproof pan and bake for 20 to 30 minutes, until soft. Remove and cool.

Squeeze the softened garlic cloves from their peel into the bowl of an electric mixer.

Add potatoes, basil, 1 Tbsp. olive oil, cream and butter and beat with the mixer until very smooth. (If potatoes appear dry, thin with more cream.)

Add cheese, salt and pepper to taste.

Serves: 4
Cost: Inexpensive
Preparation time: 45 minutes

Bartlett Pear Strudel
with Whidbeys Cream

Preheat oven to 375° F.

In a large bowl, blend the brown and white sugars and flour.

Add raisins, walnuts, nutmeg, cinnamon, orange zest and salt and mix thoroughly; mix in pears.

Lightly butter 5 sheets of phyllo dough and place them in a stack.

Spread ⅓ of the pear filling down the center and roll up in log fashion.

Repeat the process—there's enough filling for 3 logs.

Place on a lightly buttered baking sheet.

Butter or egg-wash the top and bake for 30 minutes, or until golden brown.

Cool, then cut in 2" slices and serve with Whidbeys Cream, or dust with powdered sugar.

Whidbeys Cream

Whip fresh cream until stiff, then fold into sour cream until smooth.

Stir in lemon juice, sugar and liqueur.

Serves: 6
Cost: Inexpensive
Preparation time: 60 minutes
Wine suggestion: Whidbeys Loganberry Liqueur

Pear Strudel

½ cup packed brown sugar

¼ cup white sugar

½ cup flour

½ cup Sultana (golden) raisins, soaked for 20 minutes in ½ cup Late Harvest White Riesling

½ cup chopped walnuts or hazelnuts

⅛ tsp. nutmeg

⅛ tsp. cinnamon

1 Tbsp. grated orange zest

Pinch of salt

4 pears, peeled, cored and thinly sliced

4 Tbsp. butter, softened

1 one-pound package phyllo dough

¼ cup powdered sugar (optional)

Egg Wash

1 egg whipped with ¼ cup water

Whidbeys Cream

1 pint whipping cream

⅓ cup sour cream

Juice of 1 lemon

2 Tbsp. powdered sugar

2 ounces Whidbeys Loganberry Liqueur

Apple Custard Mousse with Cherries

MOUSSE

MOUSSE

1¼ cups milk

½ cup sugar

6 egg yolks

¼ cup cold water

1 Tbsp. gelatin

1 cup whipping cream

1 Tbsp. Calvados
(apple brandy)

SWEET APPLE PUREE

2 medium Braeburn,
Jonathan or Golden
Delicious apples,
cored, peeled and
thinly sliced

1 Tbsp. lemon juice

½ cup sugar

¼ cup Late Harvest
White Riesling

MOUSSE

Over medium heat, warm milk in saucepan, then add sugar and stir until dissolved.

Whisk egg yolks lightly.

Continue to whisk while adding 3 Tbsp. sugared milk to yolks, then pour egg mixture into milk and stir until smooth.

Cook until mixture coats spoon, about 7 minutes, stirring constantly.

Pour cold water into a small bowl, sprinkle in gelatin and soften for 5 minutes.

Stir gelatin mix into warm custard, then chill over ice.

In a separate bowl, whip cream until firm, then stir in Calvados.

When custard begins to firm, fold in whipped cream, pour into buttered mold and chill for 6 hours.

Unmold the mousse, and top with either Sweet Apple Puree or Cherry Topping or both.

SWEET APPLE PUREE

In a blender or food processor, puree apples, lemon juice, sugar and Late Harvest White Riesling.

In a large saucepan, bring water to a boil, then add sugars, port, orange zest and cinnamon and boil slowly for 3 minutes.

Blend cornstarch with 1 Tbsp. water and stir into boiling sugar water.

When thickened, add cherries.

SERVES: 4
COST: INEXPENSIVE
PREPARATION TIME: 60 MINUTES
WINE SUGGESTION: LATE HARVEST WHITE RIESLING

CHERRY
TOPPING

1 cup water

½ cup sugar

¼ cup packed brown sugar

1 cup Whidbeys Port

1 Tbsp. grated orange zest

1 cinnamon stick

1 Tbsp. cornstarch

4 cups pitted sweet cherries (frozen or canned)

WINTER

ON THE PREVIOUS PAGE:
Friday Harbor Seafood Stew

Winter meals take on the scale of celebration. Although the entrees of winter don't necessarily take more time to prepare, they do require more time to cook. But we are rewarded for that extra work by the aromas of such dishes as oven-roasted turkey with rosemary, Pacific Coast Dungeness crab cakes with onions and apples, or seafood stew. ▶ When it's cold outside, Pacific Northwest menus tend to feature foods that are heavier than those offered in the warm months. By blending ginger root, curry, coconut and other ingredients from around the world with local onions, a cup or two of Dry Riesling, garlic and fresh basil, local cooks can make lamb and veal shanks a uniquely Pacific Northwest experience. ▶ Shellfish are available throughout the year. But when the water gets cold, and the breeding cycle is over, Dungeness crab reach their peak of flavor and texture.

The same can be said of local Penn Cove mussels and steamer clams. When these shellfish are simmered together with onion, butter, a full-bodied Chardonnay and aromatic vegetables, life gets just a little bit better. ❯ The cherries and berries we froze during the summer are waiting for us. A favorite dessert at our house is loganberry preserves poured over a chocolate torte. Recipes change with the season: the cherry sauce we made during the summer is lighter than the sauce prepared with the freeze-dried cherries available in late fall and winter. ❯ To accompany the season's heartier meals, full, rich Pacific Northwest Merlots and Cabernet Sauvignons are released. And the celebratory feeling of the season is capped off by cold, crisp sparkling wine.

Fresh in Winter

Seafood

Dungeness Crab

Scallops

Oysters

King Salmon

Mussels

Halibut

Clams

Meats

Pork

Venison

Beef

Duck

Pheasant

Vegetables and Root Crops

Rutabaga

Turnips

Squash

Swiss Chard

Mustard Greens

Sautéed Olympia Oysters

2 Tbsp. peanut oil

2 cloves garlic, mashed

1 Tbsp. chopped
fresh ginger root

⅓ cup Dry Riesling

2 Tbsp. lemon juice

1 tsp. chopped
fresh cilantro

Splash of chili oil

Splash of sesame oil

1 pint shelled extra
small (Olympia)
oysters

1 small jar of
pickled ginger

1 lemon, cut in wedges

Heat a heavy skillet to medium-high, add peanut oil and sauté garlic and ginger until garlic is just soft.

Reduce heat to medium, then add Dry Riesling, lemon juice, cilantro, and chili and sesame oils. Stir and simmer until well blended.

Add oysters and stir until they begin to turn color (do not overcook).

Serve in soup bowls and garnish with pickled ginger and lemon wedges.

Serves: 4
Cost: Moderate
Preparation time: 20 minutes
Wine suggestion: Dry Riesling

DUNGENESS
CRAB CAKES

In a large mixing bowl combine crab meat, red pepper, tarragon, parsley, onion, apple, lemon juice, Tabasco and mayonnaise, then season with white pepper and salt to taste.

Roll crab mix in 1½" balls, flatten to ¾", and lightly coat both sides with bread crumbs.

Heat a heavy frying pan to medium, add butter and sauté crab cakes on both sides until lightly browned.

SERVES: 4
COST: MODERATE
PREPARATION TIME: 30 MINUTES
WINE SUGGESTION: CHARDONNAY

½ pound Dungeness crab meat

1 small red bell pepper, cored and diced

1 Tbsp. chopped fresh tarragon

1 Tbsp. chopped fresh Italian parsley

1 small yellow onion, grated

1 small Granny Smith apple, peeled, cored and grated

1 tsp. lemon juice

Splash of Tabasco sauce

½ cup mayonnaise

½ tsp. finely ground white pepper

Salt

1 cup fine dry bread crumbs

2 Tbsp. butter

Antipasto with Cabernet Sauvignon Dressing

DRESSING

1 cup Cabernet Sauvignon

1 Tbsp. balsamic vinegar

Splash of Worcestershire sauce

½ clove garlic, chopped and mashed

½ cup extra virgin olive oil

1 Tbsp. chopped fresh oregano

1 Tbsp. chopped fresh marjoram

2 Tbsp. chopped fresh Italian parsley

1 tsp. dry mustard

½ tsp. sugar

½ tsp. medium-grind black pepper

Salt

ANTIPASTO

1 head butter lettuce

1 head red lettuce

1 cup roast meat, julienned

1 small white onion, sliced thin

1 red bell pepper, roasted (see page 40) and sliced

1 medium zucchini, sliced

¼ pound grated Asiago cheese

1 can black olives

DRESSING

In a small saucepan, reduce Cabernet Sauvignon by half.

Add vinegar, Worcestershire sauce and garlic.

Simmer until garlic is soft, then cool.

With a whisk, mix in olive oil, oregano, marjoram, parsley, dry mustard, sugar and pepper, then salt to taste. Mix well.

ANTIPASTO

Separate, wash and drain lettuces.

In large chilled salad bowl, mix lettuce, meat, onion, roasted pepper, zucchini, cheese and olives.

Just before serving, toss with Cabernet Sauvignon Dressing.

SERVES: 4
COST: INEXPENSIVE
PREPARATION TIME: 30 MINUTES
WINE SUGGESTION: CABERNET SAUVIGNON

CABBAGE and CRANBERRY SALAD

Add olive oil to a hot skillet and sauté cabbage and onion for 5 minutes, stirring constantly.

Add cranberries and clove and turn heat to low.

Cover and simmer 5 minutes.

Turn off heat.

In a small bowl, whisk together vinegar and sugar until well blended.

Salt to taste.

Pour vinegar over warm cabbage and toss.

Serve warm.

SERVES: 4
COST: INEXPENSIVE
PREPARATION TIME: 20 MINUTES
WINE SUGGESTION: JOHANNISBERG RIESLING

2 Tbsp. pure olive oil

1 head green cabbage, grated or thinly sliced

1 yellow onion, thinly sliced

1½ cups fresh cranberries

1 clove

2 Tbsp. white wine vinegar

2 Tbsp. sugar

Salt

Yellow Potato Leek Soup

1 Tbsp. pure olive oil

1 Tbsp. butter

2 yellow onions, thinly sliced

3 leeks, cleaned and chopped

3 cloves garlic, chopped

2 quarts chicken stock

½ cup Sauvignon Blanc

1 bay leaf

6 yellow (Finn) potatoes, peeled and quartered

¼ tsp. medium-grind black pepper

Salt

2 Tbsp. chopped fresh marjoram

Heat a heavy-gauge pot to medium, add olive oil and butter, then sauté onions, leeks and garlic until soft.

Add chicken stock, Sauvignon Blanc, bay leaf, potatoes and pepper.

Reduce heat to medium-low, cover and simmer until potatoes are very soft.

In a blender or food processor, puree the potato mixture.

Add salt to taste, then blend again.

Serve hot, garnished with marjoram.

SERVES: 8
COST: INEXPENSIVE
PREPARATION TIME: 30 MINUTES
WINE SUGGESTION: SAUVIGNON BLANC

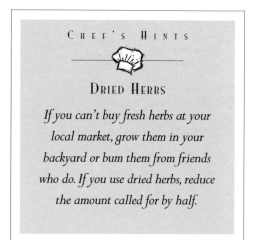

CHEF'S HINTS

DRIED HERBS

If you can't buy fresh herbs at your local market, grow them in your backyard or bum them from friends who do. If you use dried herbs, reduce the amount called for by half.

Port Chatham Smoked Salmon and Capers Pasta

Heat a heavy skillet to medium-high, then add olive oil and sauté onion until very soft.

Add garlic and sauté until garlic is just soft.

Reduce heat to medium and add tomatoes, lemon juice and Dry Riesling.

Reduce heat to low, cover and simmer until tomatoes are well cooked and saucelike.

Stir in basil, celery leaves, parsley, capers, red pepper flakes and salmon.

Simmer uncovered for 15 minutes, until sauce thickens.

In a large pot, bring 1½ quarts water to a boil, add linguine and cook for 12–15 minutes, then drain.

Place linguine in a serving dish and cover with smoked salmon sauce.

Sprinkle with Parmesan cheese and garnish with parsley.

¼ cup pure olive oil

2 onions, chopped

3 cloves garlic, mashed

2 cups chopped Roma tomatoes

Juice of ½ lemon

½ cup Dry Riesling

2 Tbsp. chopped fresh basil leaves

2 Tbsp. chopped celery leaves

2 Tbsp. chopped fresh Italian parsley

1 Tbsp. capers

Pinch of red pepper flakes

½ cup chopped hard-smoked salmon

1 pound linguine

¼ cup grated Parmesan cheese

1 sprig Italian parsley

SERVES: 4
COST: MODERATE
PREPARATION TIME: 45 MINUTES
WINE SUGGESTION: DRY RIESLING

Veal Risotto with Porcini Mushrooms

2 Tbsp. pure olive oil

2 extra large onions, finely chopped

1 fennel bulb, finely chopped

¼ cup finely chopped celery tops with leaves

2 Tbsp. chopped fresh Italian parsley

1 Tbsp. chopped fresh thyme

2 cloves garlic, chopped

½ pound ground veal or finely chopped chicken breast meat

2 Tbsp. tomato paste

2 quarts hot chicken or veal stock

½ cup dried porcini mushrooms, soaked in warm water for 45 minutes, drained and chopped

1 large head radicchio, chopped

2 cups Arborio rice

Whole nutmeg for grating

1 clove

½ tsp. medium-grind black pepper

Salt

Parmesan cheese

Green and black olives

Heat a large heavy-gauge pot to medium, add olive oil, then sauté the onion and fennel until very soft, at least 25 minutes; stir occasionally.

Reduce heat to medium-low, and add celery, parsley, thyme and garlic; cover and simmer for 20 minutes.

Increase heat to medium, add veal and continue to simmer until the meat is very tender, about 20 to 25 minutes.

Stir in tomato paste, then add 1 cup stock; cover and cook over medium heat until it begins to look like a light gravy.

Add mushrooms and radicchio and stir until the radicchio is quite wilted.

Add rice and simmer over low heat until rice has absorbed the liquid.

Add grated nutmeg (about ½ of a whole nutmeg) and the clove.

Add stock to the rice 1 cup at a time, and continue to stir rice over medium-high heat until all stock is absorbed and rice is tender.

Add pepper and salt to taste.

Serve with grated Parmesan cheese and green and black olives.

Serves: 4
Cost: Moderate
Preparation time: 60 minutes
Wine suggestions: Cabernet Sauvignon, Merlot

Beef Tenderloin with Cabernet Sauvignon and Juniper Berry Sauce

Tenderloin

Rub tenderloins with olive oil, then sprinkle with pepper and salt.

Pat on herbs and let stand while preparing sauce. (This also works well with venison.)

Cabernet Sauce

Heat heavy skillet to medium-high.

Add butter and sauté onion and garlic until very soft.

Reduce heat to medium, sprinkle in flour and stir until flour thickens.

Add Cabernet Sauvignon and veal stock.

Increase heat to medium-high. Bring sauce to a boil; reduce heat to medium and stir in Worcestershire sauce, rosemary, parsley, thyme, dry mustard, orange zest and sugar.

Mix well, then add juniper berries and cranberries and cook until the juniper berries are very soft and the sauce has been reduced by a third.

Set oven to "broil"; set temperature to 550° F.

Place tenderloins on broiler pan on the top rack of oven; broil about 7 minutes a side.

Remove from oven, drench with sauce and serve immediately.

Serves: 4
Cost: Moderate
Preparation time: 60 minutes
Wine suggestion: Cabernet Sauvignon

Tenderloin

4 six-ounce beef tenderloins

2 Tbsp. pure olive oil

½ tsp. finely ground black pepper

½ tsp. salt

¼ tsp. finely chopped fresh rosemary

¼ tsp. finely chopped fresh Italian parsley

¼ tsp. finely chopped fresh thyme

Cabernet Sauce

3 Tbsp. butter

1 yellow onion, finely chopped

1 clove garlic, finely chopped

1 Tbsp. flour

½ cup Cabernet Sauvignon

1 cup veal stock

Splash of Worcestershire sauce

¼ tsp. finely chopped fresh rosemary

¼ tsp. finely chopped fresh Italian parsley

¼ tsp. finely chopped fresh thyme

¼ tsp. dry mustard

¼ tsp. grated orange zest

1 tsp. sugar

2 Tbsp. juniper berries

½ cup fresh cranberries

Oregon Blue Cheese Stuffed Flank Steak with Mushroom Sauce

Meat Seasoning

2 Tbsp. extra virgin olive oil

2 Tbsp. Cabernet Sauvignon

Splash of Worcestershire sauce

2 cloves garlic, chopped

1 Tbsp. chopped fresh Italian parsley

1 Tbsp. chopped fresh rosemary

1 Tbsp. chopped fresh thyme

½ tsp. medium-grind black pepper

Salt

Meat Seasoning

In a small bowl mix olive oil, Cabernet Sauvignon, Worcestershire sauce, garlic, parsley, rosemary, thyme and pepper.

Mix thoroughly, then salt to taste.

Stuffing

Preheat oven to 350° F.

Fillet steak open and thoroughly rub on both sides with meat seasoning, then lay flat on cutting board to rest for 45 minutes at room temperature.

In large bowl, mix spinach, eggs, bread crumbs, cheese, olive oil, vinegar, pine nuts, mushrooms and garlic, then salt to taste.

Spread spinach mixture evenly over the steak.

Roll up steak loosely and tie with kitchen string.

Heat a large skillet to medium-high, add olive oil and butter, then quickly brown the steak on both sides.

Remove to ovenproof dish and bake for 25 minutes.

Add the shallots to the pan in which you browned the meat, and quickly sauté until transparent.

Deglaze pan with Cabernet Sauvignon.

Add veal stock, Worcestershire sauce, sugar, salt and mushrooms.

Reduce heat to medium and simmer for 10 minutes, or until reduced and slightly thickened.

Slice steak (¾") and lay flat on serving plate. Top with Mushroom Sauce.

SERVES: 6
COST: MODERATE TO EXPENSIVE
PREPARATION TIME: 90 MINUTES
WINE SUGGESTION: CABERNET SAUVIGNON

STUFFING

3-pound flank steak

2 packages frozen chopped spinach, thawed and drained

2 eggs

2 Tbsp. fine fresh bread crumbs

¼ pound blue cheese, crumbled

2 Tbsp. extra virgin olive oil

Splash balsamic vinegar

2 Tbsp. pine nuts, roasted

¼ cup dried porcini mushrooms, soaked in warm water for 45 minutes, drained and finely chopped

1 clove garlic, chopped

Salt

1 Tbsp. pure olive oil

1 Tbsp. butter

MUSHROOM SAUCE

2 Tbsp. chopped shallots

½ cup Cabernet Sauvignon

¼ cup veal stock

Splash of Worcestershire sauce

Pinch of sugar

Pinch of salt

¼ cup chopped portobello mushrooms

Sausage-Stuffed Fresh Roast Turkey

Sausage
Stuffing

2 Tbsp. pure olive oil

2 Tbsp. butter

1 large onion, chopped

2 cloves garlic, chopped

1 pound mildly seasoned Italian sausage

¼ cup chopped celery tops

1 Granny Smith apple, peeled, cored and cubed

1 package frozen chopped spinach, thawed and drained

1 tsp. chopped fresh rosemary

1 tsp. chopped fresh thyme

1 Tbsp. chopped fresh sage

1 Tbsp. chopped fresh Italian parsley

2 cups cubed dry bread

2 cups chicken stock

2 Tbsp. Dry Riesling

Sausage Stuffing

Heat a large heavy skillet to medium.

Add olive oil and butter, then add onion and garlic and sauté until soft.

Add sausage, break up and cook until just done.

Remove from heat and cool.

Add celery, apple, spinach, rosemary, thyme, sage, parsley and bread cubes, then mix thoroughly.

Stir in chicken stock and Dry Riesling.

(Note: Stuffing should be moist but not mushy.)

Turkey Basting

Combine olive oil, lemon juice, garlic, Dry Riesling, parsley, rosemary, thyme, sage and pepper in a blender, then salt to taste.

Turkey

Preheat oven to 425° F.

Rinse turkey, inside and out, under cold water and dry.

Just before roasting, stuff turkey cavities with Sausage Stuffing (do not pack stuffing too tightly).

Close cavity using metal skewers, or sew up with cooking twine.

Tie legs together.

Place turkey on a rack in a roasting pan, immediately put in oven and reduce oven temperature to 350° F.

Bake turkey for 4½ hours, basting frequently.

SERVES: 8
COST: MODERATE
PREPARATION TIME: ALL DAY, BUT IT'S FUN
WINE SUGGESTIONS: DRY RIESLING, MERLOT

TURKEY BASTING

2 Tbsp. pure olive oil

Juice of 2 lemons

4 cloves garlic

¼ cup Dry Riesling

1 tsp. chopped fresh Italian parsley

1 tsp. chopped fresh rosemary

1 tsp. chopped fresh thyme

1 tsp. chopped fresh sage

½ tsp. medium-grind black pepper

Salt

TURKEY

14-pound fresh turkey

CHEF'S HINTS

ROASTING MEATS

It's best to let meat warm to room temperature before roasting. When marinating meat, one hour at room temperature should do it.

Fraser River Salmon with Merlot Fennel Sauce

Merlot Fennel Sauce

1 Tbsp. pure olive oil

1 Tbsp. butter

1 medium yellow onion, chopped

1 clove garlic, chopped

1 medium fennel bulb, chopped

2 shallots, chopped

1½ cups Merlot

1 cup fish stock

2 Tbsp. chopped fresh tarragon

Pinch of sugar

Pinch of cayenne pepper

Salt

1 Tbsp. arrowroot, mixed into ¼ cup water

Salmon

4 six-ounce salmon fillets (or steaks)

2 Tbsp. pure olive oil

½ tsp. finely ground white pepper

Salt

Juice of ½ lemon

Merlot Fennel Sauce

Heat heavy skillet to medium-high. Add olive oil and butter, then sauté onion, garlic, fennel and shallots until soft.

Reduce heat to medium-low, then add Merlot and simmer until reduced to ½ cup of liquid.

Increase heat to medium and add fish stock, tarragon, sugar and cayenne pepper.

Salt to taste and simmer for 5 minutes.

Add arrowroot and simmer until sauce thickens.

Salmon

Rinse salmon fillets in cold water, then pat dry.

Rub with a little of the oil, white pepper and salt.

Heat a large heavy-gauge frying pan to medium-high, add remaining olive oil, then sauté salmon 3 to 4 minutes per side.

Place salmon on heated platter, sprinkle with lemon juice, then drench with Merlot Fennel Sauce. Serve immediately.

Serves: 4
Cost: Moderate
Preparation time: 45 minutes
Wine suggestion: Merlot

Friday Harbor Seafood Stew

Heat large heavy pot to medium-high, add olive oil, then sauté onion, red and green peppers and fennel until soft.

Cover, reduce heat to low and cook for 20 minutes.

Increase heat to medium, then add celery and garlic and sauté until garlic is soft (about 5 minutes).

Add tomatoes, basil, marjoram, parsley, Sauvignon Blanc, lemon juice, black pepper and salt to taste.

Cover, reduce heat to low and cook for 20 minutes.

Add clams, scallops, mussels, crab and halibut to sauce, cover and cook for 7–10 minutes or until clams and mussels open.

Serve as a stew with toasted Italian bread or linguine.

SERVES: 6
COST: EXPENSIVE
PREPARATION TIME: 45 MINUTES
WINE SUGGESTIONS: CHARDONNAY,
SAUVIGNON BLANC

3 Tbsp. pure olive oil

1 large yellow onion, chopped

1 red bell pepper, cored and diced

1 green bell pepper, cored and diced

1 fennel bulb, chopped

2 Tbsp. finely chopped celery tops

6 cloves garlic, finely chopped

4 cups chopped Roma tomatoes

3 Tbsp. chopped fresh basil

2 Tbsp. chopped fresh marjoram

2 Tbsp. chopped fresh Italian parsley

½ cup Sauvignon Blanc

Juice of ½ lemon

1 tsp. medium-grind black pepper

Salt

1 pound steamer clams, cleaned

¼ pound scallops

2 pounds mussels, cleaned

6 crab legs, cracked

½ pound halibut, cut into ½" cubes

GREAT NORTHERN
BEAN CASSEROLE

1 pound Great
Northern beans

2 Tbsp. pure olive oil

2 slices bacon, diced

2 small yellow onions,
chopped

4 cloves garlic,
chopped

¼ cup chopped celery
tops

1 cup chopped Roma
tomatoes

1 quart chicken stock

¼ cup Sauvignon Blanc

3 Tbsp. chopped fresh
Italian parsley

3 Tbsp. chopped fresh
oregano

1 tsp. ground cumin

Pinch of red pepper
flakes

1 ham hock

Salt

Add 3 quarts water to a large pot, pour in
the beans and boil for 10 minutes.

Turn off heat, cover and let stand for 1 hour.

Heat a large heavy-gauge pot to medium-
hot, add olive oil and bacon, then sauté
onion, garlic and celery until soft.

Reduce heat to medium, then add tomatoes
and cook until very soft.

Add chicken stock, Sauvignon Blanc,
parsley, oregano, cumin, pepper flakes and
ham hock.

Drain the beans, then add to the broth. Salt
to taste.

Cover and simmer over low heat, stirring
occasionally, for 1½ hours, or until beans are
very tender.

May also be served as a rich soup.

SERVES: 8
COST: INEXPENSIVE
PREPARATION TIME: 30 MINUTES
WINE SUGGESTIONS: CABERNET SAUVIGNON, MERLOT

CHATEAU POTATOES with YAKIMA GOUDA

Preheat oven to 375° F.

In a buttered baking dish place alternating layers of potato and onion slices and grated Gouda cheese; sprinkle with black pepper and a small amount of chopped fresh oregano.

Repeat layers at least three deep.

Cover the potatoes with milk that has been heated almost to boiling.

Bake for one hour, or until top has browned and potatoes are tender.

SERVES: 6 TO 8
COST: MODERATE
PREPARATION TIME: 15 MINUTES

4 medium russet potatoes, peeled and thinly sliced

2 medium white onions, thinly sliced

⅓ pound Yakima Gouda cheese, grated

½ tsp. medium-grind black pepper

1 Tbsp. chopped fresh oregano

1 quart whole milk

GARLIC and LEEK POTATO PANCAKES

4 large russet potatoes, peeled and quartered

2 leeks, cleaned and coarsely chopped

1 bulb garlic, roasted (see page 78)

2 Tbsp. extra virgin olive oil

2 Tbsp. heavy cream

½ cup grated Parmesan cheese

½ tsp. finely ground white pepper

Salt

2 Tbsp. butter

Boil potatoes and leeks together in water to cover until potatoes are tender. Drain and cool.

Squeeze garlic into a blender or food processor and add olive oil, cream, Parmesan, pepper and salt to taste; mix.

Add potatoes and leeks and blend until smooth. (Add more cream if needed to smooth.)

Form into 8 patties and fry in butter until browned.

SERVES: 6 TO 8
COST: INEXPENSIVE
PREPARATION TIME: 20 MINUTES

Chocolate Torte with Loganberry Preserves

Preheat oven to 400° F.

Line two 8" springform pans with parchment.

In a double boiler, melt chocolate and butter. (Do not overheat.)

Fold eggs into chocolate and butter.

Stir in liqueur and orange zest and immediately pour into the springform pans.

Place pans in warm water bath and bake for 15 minutes.

Remove from oven and cool.

Remove tortes from pans.

Spread loganberry preserves over one cake, then place second cake on top.

Chill in refrigerator for two hours.

Just before serving, top with Whidbeys Cream (see page 79).

1 pound bittersweet chocolate

½ pound unsalted butter

6 eggs, whipped

3 ounces Whidbeys Loganberry Liqueur

1 tsp. grated orange zest

Loganberry preserves

SERVES: 6
COST: MODERATE, IF YOU ALREADY HAVE THE LIQUEUR
PREPARATION TIME: 30 MINUTES
WINE SUGGESTION: PORT

Poached Pears with Caramel Nut Topping

Pears

3 Anjou pears

1 cup Late Harvest White Riesling

1 clove

2 thin slices orange peel

Whipped cream

Caramel Nut Topping

2 cups water

½ cup packed brown sugar

2 Tbsp. sugar

1 tsp. grated orange zest

3 Tbsp. butter

½ cup mixed chopped nuts (e.g., hazelnuts, almonds and walnuts)

Pears

Preheat oven to 375° F.

Peel, halve and core pears.

Place pears in baking dish and add Late Harvest White Riesling, clove and orange peel.

Cover and bake for 15 minutes, then turn pears and bake another 15 minutes, or until pears are tender; remove and cool.

To serve, place pear half on plate—core side up—and fill with Caramel Nut Topping.

Top with whipped cream.

Caramel Nut Topping

In saucepan boil water, then add brown and white sugars, orange zest and butter, stirring constantly until mixture thickens (about 10 minutes).

Remove from heat and stir in nuts.

Serves: 6
Cost: Inexpensive
Preparation time: 60 minutes
Wine suggestion: Late Harvest White Riesling

THE
WELL-EQUIPPED
KITCHEN

Asian Pantry

Basics

Rice: Short-Grain,
Regular White
and Pearl

Selection of Asian
Dried Noodles

Dried Forest
Mushrooms

Canned Water
Chestnuts

Canned Bamboo
Shoots

Almonds

Rice Paper Sheets

Chicken Stock

Cornstarch

Peanuts

Yellow Onions

Garlic (fresh)

Ginger (fresh)

Fortune Cookies

Green Onions

Coconut Milk

Peanut Oil

Sesame Oil

Pepper Oil

Rice Wine Vinegar

Soy Sauce

Wasabe (Green
Horseradish)

Asian Fish Sauce

Pickled Ginger

Oyster Sauce

Teriyaki Sauce

Hot Red Pepper
Sauce or Paste

Peanut Sauce

Thai Fish Sauce

Black Bean Sauce

Sesame Seeds

Frozen Peas

Herbs/Spices

Red Pepper Flakes

Cumin

Curry

Ginger

Anise

Chinese Five Spice

Coriander

Turmeric

Dry Mustard

Italian–Mediterranean Pantry

Basics

Selection of Dried Pastas

Dried Beans: Cannellini, Great Northern, Lentils

Canned Garbanzo Beans

Tomato Paste

Canned Italian Plum Tomatoes

Tomato Sauce

Chicken Stock

Canned Anchovy Paste

Canned Tuna in Olive Oil

Canned Sweet Red Peppers

Olives

Dried Porcini Mushrooms

Sun-Dried Tomatoes

Capers

Yellow Onions

Garlic (fresh)

Shallots

Olive Oil (Pure and Extra Virgin)

Worcestershire Sauce

Tabasco Sauce

Red Wine Vinegar

White Wine Vinegar

Balsamic Vinegar

Arborio Rice

Pine Nuts

Dijon Mustard

Polenta

Herbs/Spices

Cumin

Oregano

Basil

Bay Leaf

Sage

Thyme

Red Pepper Flakes

Black Peppercorns

Dry Mustard

Rosemary

Refrigerator

Cheese: Parmesan, Gorgonzola, Mozzarella

Pesto

Roma Tomatoes

AMERICAN PANTRY

BASICS

Kidney Beans

Tuna

Chicken and
Beef Broth

Ketchup

Mustards
(Yellow, Dijon)

Lentils

Mayonnaise

Honey

Oatmeal

Bread Crumbs

Refried Beans

Barbecue Sauce

Relish

Jam

Red and White
Wine Vinegar

Worcestershire
Sauce

Tabasco

Onions

Garlic

Crackers

Chocolate Chips

Raisins

Nuts (variety)

White Sugar

Brown Sugar

Baking Powder

Baking Soda

Yeast

Pancake Mix

Potatoes

HERBS/SPICES

Rosemary

Thyme

Oregano

Basil

Sage

Chili Powder

Dry Mustard

Celery Seed

Cinnamon

Nutmeg

Allspice

REFRIGERATOR

Cheese: Cheddar,
Swiss, Jack, Gouda

Flour Tortillas

Sour Cream

Salsas

Pickles

Butter

Cured Ham

Bacon

Eggs

Cream Cheese

Sauerkraut

Celery

Parsley

Tomatoes

Lemons

Essential Utensils

POTS

Pasta Pot

12-Quart Stock Pot

6-Quart Wok

4-Quart Saucepan

2-Quart Saucepan

Sauté Pans — 6", 10", 14"

Large Dutch Oven

6" Nonstick Pan

Lids

KNIVES

8" Chef

4" Paring

4" Boning

6" Serrated

GENERAL KITCHEN GADGETS

Colander

Tongs

Wooden Spoons

Rubber Spatula

Whisk

Wire Whip

Cheese Grater

Plastic Cutting Board

Peeler

Zester

Measuring Cups and Spoons

Wire Strainer (fine mesh)

Meat Thermometer

Pepper Grinder

Pastry Bag and Tips

Rolling Pins

Blender

Cuisinart

Selection of Bowls

Plastic Storage Containers

Roasting Pan

Cookie Sheets

Hand Juicer

Mallet

Pastry Brush

CHEF'S HINTS

Avoid using metal spoons in your pots and pans.

Wine Descriptions

Cabernet Sauvignon: An intense, full-bodied, deep red wine, Cabernet Sauvignon is rich in oaky, mouth-filling flavor and reminiscent of chocolate, black cherries, raspberries and currants. Pair this wine with full-flavored or generously seasoned foods, such as pasta with red sauce, beef or game.

Chardonnay: One of the most refined and complex of white grapes, Chardonnay is the basis for some of the world's great wines. Its dry flavor has been described as a blend of apple, pear, vanilla and honey. Chateau Ste. Michelle's 100 percent oak-aged Chardonnay is barrel-fermented, with toasty, creamy characteristics, and goes well with shellfish, pheasant and veal.

Chenin Blanc: Chenin Blanc is a medium-dry, light-bodied, aromatic white wine with a hint of effervescence. Its slightly floral aroma and simple, delicate honeydew melon flavor are unmistakable when served chilled. An ideal aperitif wine served with mild and strongly flavored cheeses, appetizers and dips, Chenin Blanc also completes a meal of shellfish or poultry.

Dry Riesling: This crisp, medium-bodied white wine offers a subtle, balanced flavor. It has an aroma that recalls peaches, and its citrus flavors are most apparent to the taster's palate. When served chilled, Dry Riesling complements a broad spectrum of foods, including seafood, poultry dishes, and smoked and spicy foods.

Gewürztraminer: The grapes of this perfumed, spicy wine have found a home in the Columbia Valley's cooler, sloped vineyards, which are reminiscent of those of Alsace, France. Medium-dry Gewürztraminer is an ideal complement to mild cheeses, poultry, duck and pork.

JOHANNISBERG RIESLING: Also known as White Riesling, this is a medium-dry wine with a crisp, delicate palate. Longer time on the vine and special handling during fermentation and aging produce rich, complex fruit flavors such as peach and apricot. It complements a range of foods, from light cream-based sauces to grilled seafood and smoked foods.

LATE HARVEST WHITE RIESLING: This rich, nectarlike dessert wine is fermented from grapes thick with "the noble rot," botrytis. Well balanced and high in residual sugar, Late Harvest White Riesling ages well in the bottle. Its aromatic blend of honey, peaches, apricots, pears and orange peels makes it the perfect accompaniment to desserts such as poached apples or pears.

MERLOT: Although it possesses the same barrel character as Cabernet Sauvignon, Merlot is softer and more subtle. This French grape has adapted well to Washington's growing conditions. After slowly aging in oak barrels, Merlot develops a rich fragrance and full body with a deep aroma reminiscent of black cherries. It goes well with pasta with red sauce, game birds and lamb.

PINOT NOIR: The basis for both the French burgundies and the sparkling wines of Champagne, this small red grape produces a medium-bodied, dry red wine with a spicy, earthy flavor. Pinot Noir can be paired with strongly flavored cheeses, salmon and various meat dishes.

SAUVIGNON BLANC: This crisp, full-bodied white wine recalls tropical fruit, such as melon, pineapple and banana, and citrus fruit, such as grapefruit and lemon. Sauvignon Blanc's qualities complement a wide range of foods, including shellfish, seafood in light sauces, grilled fish and poultry.

SEMILLON: Chateau Ste. Michelle's Semillon achieves a body and complexity on a par with those of grapes produced in Bordeaux. A crisp, dry, subtly fragrant wine with a hint of lemon and figs, Semillon goes with clams, mussels, oysters, grilled fish, pasta with cream sauce and a variety of Asian foods.

GUIDE to FOOD and WINE PAIRING

Mild Cheeses
Strongly Flavored Cheeses
Appetizers, Dips
Oysters
Shrimp, Crab, Lobster
Clams, Mussels
Seafood with wine or light sauces
Seafood with cream sauces
Grilled Fish
Salmon
Pasta with cream sauce
Pasta with red sauce
Poultry
Pheasant, Duck, Goose
Asian Food
Pork, Veal
Lamb
Game
Beef
Fruit and Light Desserts
Chocolate Desserts

These wine and food pairings are only suggestions. Individual taste is the ultimate guide to food and wine combinations.

	gnon	Zinfandel	White Riesling	Late Harvest White Riesling	Late Harvest Sauvignon Blanc	Port	Extra Dry	Champagne Brut	Blanc de Blanc	Blanc de Noir
				Sweet						
		◗					◗	◗	◗	
			◗	◗	◗		◗	◗	◗	◗
							◗	◗	◗	◗
								◗	◗	◗
								◗	◗	◗
								◗	◗	◗
							◗	◗	◗	◗
							◗	◗	◗	◗
							◗	◗	◗	
		◗	◗	◗			◗	◗	◗	◗
					◗					

Guide to Wine and Herb/Spice Pairing

	Herbs	Spices
Chenin Blanc	Anise, Chervil, Cilantro, Dill, Fennel, Lemon Thyme, Parsley	Allspice, Cloves, Nutmeg
Dry Riesling	Chervil, Cilantro, Fennel, Parsley, Sage	Allspice, Chili Powder, Curry, Ginger, Nutmeg
Gewürztraminer	Cilantro, Mint	Black Pepper, Curry, Fennel Seeds, Ginger, Nutmeg
Johannisberg Riesling	Chervil, Coriander Seeds, Dill, Parsley	Allspice, Black Pepper, Cloves, Ginger, Mace, Nutmeg
Chardonnay	Mustard Seeds, Rosemary, Sage, Tarragon	Cloves, Fresh Ginger, Orange Zest
Sauvignon Blanc	Basil, Bay Leaf, Garlic, Oregano, Rosemary, Savory, Thyme	Black Pepper, Cumin, Ginger
Semillon	Basil, Dill, Lemon Thyme, Summer Savory	Cumin, Ginger, Sweet Paprika
Pinot Noir	Mint, Rosemary, Sage, Thyme	Allspice, Nutmeg, Pink Peppercorns
Cabernet Sauvignon	Bay Leaf, Marjoram, Parsley, Rosemary, Thyme	Allspice, Mace, Nutmeg
Merlot	Basil, Oregano, Rosemary, Thyme	Allspice, Mace, Nutmeg, Star Anise

INDEX

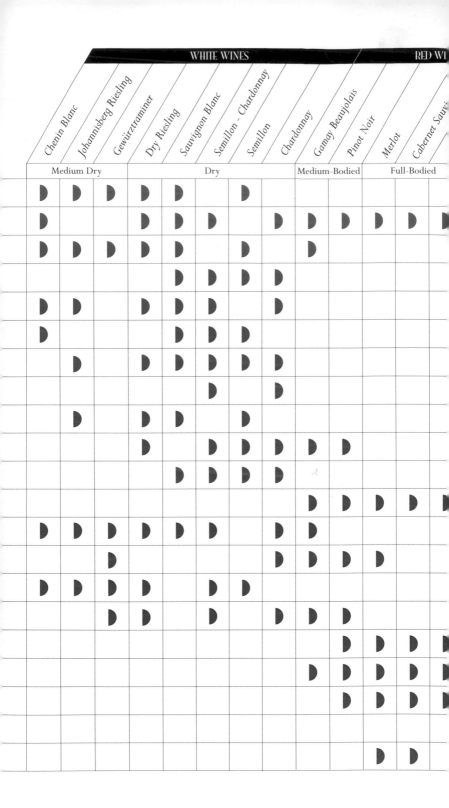